P9-DGU-419

the IMPACT of the FUTURE

the IMPACT of the FUTURE

Lyle E. Schaller

abingdon press ⓟ *nashville and new york*

THE IMPACT OF THE FUTURE

Copyright © 1969 by Abingdon Press

All rights in this book are reserved.
No part of the book may be reproduced in any
manner whatsoever without written permission of
the publishers except brief quotations embodied in
critical articles or reviews. For information address
Abingdon Press, Nashville, Tennessee.

Standard Book Number: 687-18699-4
Library of Congress Catalog Card Number: 69-18455

Parts of Chapter 18 are reprinted from "The
Challenge of Creative Federalism" by Lyle E.
Schaller. Copyright 1967 Christian Century
Foundation. Reprinted by permission from the
May 10, 1967 issue of *The Christian Century*.

SET UP, PRINTED, AND BOUND BY THE
PARTHENON PRESS, AT NASHVILLE,
TENNESSEE, UNITED STATES OF AMERICA

260
Sch 2

Baker & Taylor

3 33⁻

19 June 49

32414

TO
Walter
John
Rebecca
Robert
Laura
and
David

CONTENTS

PART FIVE
THREE TRENDS IN THE
RELIGIOUS ARENA

INTRODUCTION

John Alan Rogers was born on May 22, 1952.

A straight linear projection of the 1950-60 trend shows that when Johnny reaches his twenty-third birthday all but a few hundred farmers will have disappeared from the American scene.

A straight linear projection of the changes that occurred between 1900 and 1950 in the length of the work week indicate that when John Rogers reaches his sixty-second birthday the work week will be down to zero hours.

A projection of the 1957 to 1966 trend suggests that in the same year that John celebrates his fortieth birthday the last baby to be baptized in the Presbyterian Church U.S. will receive the sacrament of baptism.

A projection of the 1940-66 changes indicates that about

the time John's first grandchild is born every mother with a child under the age of eighteen will be employed outside the home.

A projection of the 1939-65 changes in the life expectancy of men and women reveals that John's wife will live 18 years after his death.

An extrapolation of the expenditures of the national government for research and development from 1945 to 1965 indicates that by the time John Rogers reaches his twenty-seventh birthday the federal investment in research and development will require the entire federal budget and that by the time John is fifty-three years old the entire gross national product will be devoted to this effort.

Do these statements startle you? They should. Before jumping to any conclusions, however, it might be helpful to look more carefully at these projections.

First of all, each one of these statements is literally true; but this does not mean that these are reliable predictions about the future. It would be more helpful to begin each paragraph with the qualifying phrase, "*If* the trend that developed between these years continues, *and if* no new force comes into play to modify this trend, thus and so will happen." In each one of these statements a couple of mighty big qualifying ifs are present.

Second, these examples illustrate the need to be very careful about taking trends and simply projecting them into the future. Common sense tells us that probably none of the eventualities suggested in the opening paragraphs will occur.

Third, despite the qualifications these statements do help to dramatize the tremendous changes that are occurring in American society. These statements also help us to begin to grasp the magnitude of the changes that will occur during the lifetime of a person born near the middle of the twentieth century.

Fourth, any churchman looking at these and other projections into the future should see that the direction and pace of change will affect the role, the responsibilities, and the ministry of the churches.

This book is based on the assumption that an effective and relevant strategy for a local church, for a denominational agency, or for interchurch cooperation *must* take into account those trends that will influence the execution of the church's plans. This means that churchmen should develop a greater interest in the future and in what the future may bring. This is a relatively new concept. It is an idea that gains far more support in words than in action. It is a statement that is easy to agree with, but difficult to implement. It is an argument that has great surface attraction, but in fact runs counter to the attitudes, practices, traditions, and habits of most adults over thirty years of age.

Traditionally man has not displayed a strong interest in the future. He has shown a far greater interest in the past than in the future. In the United States there are literally scores of associations, societies, and clubs concerned with the past. Many of these have been in existence for several decades. By contrast, the World Future Society, the only professional organization in the country specifically formed around an orientation to the future, first came into existence in 1966.

This concern with the future is a new theme in American life. Except for the comic strip and a few novels such as Edward Bellamy's *Looking Backward,* George Orwell's *1984,* Nevil Shute's *On the Beach,* and Aldous Huxley's *Brave New World,* Americans have expressed relatively little interest in the future.

A perusal of the periodicals published in the late 1890's and the early years of this century reveals very few articles forecasting what life would be like in the new century. Although the world was standing on the front edge of a new century there appeared to be little interest in predicting what life would be like in 1950 or 2000. The forecasts that were made tended to follow a "more of the same, only bigger and better" theme. They were limited largely to a projection of existing trends, and there was little awareness of the changes that would sharply alter a simple straight-line projection of existing trends.

There were a few exceptions to this. In a series of articles in *The North American Review* in 1901 H. G. Wells predicted, "Long before the year 2000 A.D., probably before 1950, a successful aeroplane will have soared and come home safe and sound. Directly that is accomplished, the new invention will be most assuredly applied to war." In this same series Wells also predicted the development of the electric range for cooking and the suburbanization and decentralization of the urban population.

In an address to the graduating class of the Yale Law School on June 24, 1895, the lawyer Henry B. Brown forecast that the twentieth century would bring the further development of the two great inventions of the era—steam for transportation and electricity for the transmission of intelligence. He predicted a continued trend toward consolidation in politics, business, and society, and a continued centralization of power. He saw that the reconciliation of conflict between labor and management would become one of the great problems of the twentieth century. In looking at the world scene he forecast that by the year A.D. 2000 the Eastern hemisphere would be under the control of the colonial powers of the West.

An examination of a score of different forecasts about the new century reveals several interesting patterns. Many saw the elimination of poverty; the necessity of eliminating the slums; and the development of the radio, motion pictures, and television. No one mentioned race relations as a problem that might become a major issue in the twentieth century. No one predicted the surge of nationalism that would dominate international relations in the middle of the twentieth century. These forecasters tended to overlook the gasoline engine and predicted that electricity would be the prime source of motive power for land transportation. They completely missed the decline of manufacturing as a source of employment and failed to see the rise of the service trades as a major source of employment. A few saw the problem of air pollution on the horizon, but no one mentioned the matter of water pollution.

As one should expect, most of those looking into the twentieth century saw the disappearance of that which they disliked. A lady prohibitionist predicted the elimination of alcoholic beverages. An anti-union businessman forecast the disappearance of labor unions.

If the judgment of the editors of periodicals published back at the turn of the century reflected the attitude of the people, there was far more interest in the past and in the present than in the future.

Today, with the end of the century only three decades away, there is rapidly developing a much greater interest in the future. There is a growing number of research organizations such as the Hudson Institute, the Rand Corporation, and the Urban Institute that have been set up to define the issues and to study the problems of tomorrow.

The American Institute of Planners, founded in 1916, organized a two-year consultation on "The Next Fifty Years" to celebrate its fiftieth anniversary. One of the products of that was the book *Environment for Man: The Next Fifty Years,* edited by William R. Ewald, Jr. One could point to a variety of other future-oriented projects, ranging from the Committee on the Next Thirty Years of the English Social

Science Research Council, to the project "Mankind 2000" created by a group of planners from all over the world meeting in London, to the decision by the Columbia Broadcasting System to replace the documentary series "The Twentieth Century" with one on the twenty-first century. The American Academy of Arts and Science has established the Commission on the Year 2000. The summer, 1967, issue of *Daedalus,* the Journal published by the Academy, was devoted to a report on the early deliberations of the Commission. A few months later Herman Kahn and Anthony J. Wiener published their book *The Year 2000: A Framework for Speculation on the Next Thirty-three Years.* In mid-1968 a special task force in the Lutheran Church in America completed a study of the significant issues for the 1970's as part of an effort by one denomination to strengthen the churches' orientation toward tomorrow. In 1968 an economist by the name of Burnham P. Beckwith published a book in which he attempts to forecast over seventy major trends that he believes will affect people during the next five centuries (*The Next 500 Years*).

Departments of research and development or long-range planning are now well entrenched in the bureaucratic structure and the budgeting processes of most large organizations, including many of the national and regional agencies of the Christian churches.

Out of the growing concern with tomorrow a new group of specialists, the futurists, has emerged. They are using the tools developed by the social and behavioral sciences to study the future in general and the process of change in particular. It is becoming apparent to an increasing number of people that while the future begins where the present stops, change is having a much greater impact on breaking up what once was thought of as a simple pattern of continuity. The straight-line projection of past trends is now recognized as an inadequate basis for predicting the future.*

This can be illustrated by looking at the predictions of disaster made in the 1920's and 1930's. Those who used straight-line projections predicted that by 1960 the nation's supply of petroleum would be exhausted and by 1970 the coal reserves of the country would be depleted. The population projections of the 1930's (which turned out to be too low), and of the nineteen-fifties (which turned out to be too high), both relied too heavily on past trends and neglected the impact of changing social and economic conditions.

This book is an attempt to encourage churchmen to develop a more thoughtful and critical view of the future as they make the decisions today that will affect the churches of tomorrow. It was written with four objectives in mind.

The first was simply to identify twenty important trends that will affect the churches of tomorrow. For the most part these trends are limited to demographic, social, economic, political, and institutional patterns in the United States. Conspicuously absent is any mention of trends in international affairs—and these are certain to have an impact on the churches. Also omitted is any discussion of trends in theological thought. These omissions were deliberate and reflect both the limitations of space and the limitations of the author's competence.

The second objective was to describe and to analyze each of these trends and to discuss some of the factors that may shape them. Hopefully this has been done in a manner that will be helpful to the churchman who is concerned with the future and with his church's response to change.

The third purpose in writing this book was to predict some

* For an excellent criticism of efforts to forecast the future see Robert A. Nisbet, "The Year 2000 and All That," *Commentary,* June, 1968.

of the implications of these trends for the churches. With some of the trends it is possible to develop a comparatively detailed statement on the implications. With others, the future is so uncertain that it is possible only to speculate on the implications. In some cases this can be done most easily by simply posing a series of provocative questions.

The fourth objective was the most ambitious. It was to present to the people who are making the decisions about the future of the churches a handbook that (1) would bring together relevant factual data in a convenient and usable form, (2) could provide the context for more detailed studies and plans in response to specific problems, (3) would stimulate creative innovation in carrying out the ministry of the church and a greater awareness of the importance of planned change, and (4) would encourage the decision makers in the churches to believe that tomorrow will be different from yesterday, that the problems of the future will be more complex and more difficult of solution than those of the present, and that the dangers inherent in simplistic solutions and slogans will be greater tomorrow than ever before.

One of the most interesting ideas in the book *The Year 2000* by Kahn and Wiener is their speculation about how "surprise-free" the last third of this century will be. They conclude that it may have fewer surprises to disrupt projections about the future than was the case in either the first or the second third of this century. They may be right, but the reader should be warned that several of the trends described in this book, especially those in Parts Three and Four, are vulnerable to "surprise" developments that may occur in the next decade or two.

The nature of the subject matter and the organization of the material mean that it is not necessary for the reader to begin with the first chapter and end with the last chapter.

Each chapter stands alone, and, while there are cross-references to other chapters scattered through the book, the reader may begin where he wishes and proceed in any manner he wishes without sacrificing a sense of continuity.

In an effort to provide some direction for those who seek it, the contents have been divided into five parts, and related chapters have been grouped together. In the first part four chapters are devoted to trends that have become encrusted with a deceptive veneer of myths in recent years. Here an attempt has been made to look behind the stereotypes and identify and describe what appears to this writer to be reality.

In Part Two four basic trends in population changes and housing are identified and described. The reader who plans to read the entire book at one time may prefer to start with these four chapters.

Part Three consists of five of the most subjective chapters in the book. The social and economic trends reported here are more vulnerable to "surprise" developments than any others in the entire book.

In recent years the source and distribution of power in our society has become a subject of intense interest for many churchmen. In Part Four are gathered the four chapters that bear most directly on this theme.

Finally, in Part Five three trends within the institutional expression of the church are identified and described. These may be of greatest interest to the professional churchman.

Many debts were incurred in the preparation of this book, and most of them must go unacknowledged. Footnotes and other scholarly paraphernalia deliberately have been kept to a minimum. At the end of each chapter items have been listed that may be of interest to those who would like to read further about a specific trend or its implications. This list usually includes some of the major sources of information and insights for that chapter, but most of the items listed were chosen because of their potential interest to the reader.

The earliest stimulus for a project of this nature came from Richard E. Moore and E. Eugene Huff, who encouraged the preparation of a monograph on trends affecting new church development. Later I had the good fortune to work with a task force of the Ecumenical Study Commission of Ohio. The intellectual stimulation provided by Joe Duncan, John Mitchell, Fred Staub, Mrs. M. M. Triplett, and Carlton Weber shaped many of the ideas and conclusions scattered through this volume. I am most grateful for their cooperation, their insights, and their friendship.

Finally I must again acknowledge with heartfelt thanks the unparalleled opportunities provided me by the trustees of the Regional Church Planning Office.

This book is dedicated to six people from the generation that will provide the leaders for the church of the future.

PART ONE

STEREOTYPES VERSUS REALITY

1. FROM URBANIZATION
TO DECENTRALIZATION

BASIC TREND

Decentralization has replaced urbanization as the dominant characteristic of the changes in the population of the United States.

At nearly every meeting or conference that takes up the subject of the church and the urban crisis someone will emphasize the growing proportion of the population living in urban communities in the United States. Speakers make categorical statements such as "We now have become a nation of cities, and the churches must awaken to this fact," or "By their actions the American people have demonstrated an overwhelming preference for urban life."

Perhaps the most important characteristic of these two statements is that they reflect a growing body of misleading myths.

It is true that an increasing proportion of the nation's

population is being concentrated in a few urban regions. The fifteen largest multi-county urban regions—and several of them consist of two or more of what the Bureau of the Census defines as a Standard Metropolitan Statistical Area (SMSA)—include about 65,000,000 residents, or nearly one third of the nation's population. It is true that another 200 of these metropolitan areas contain another one third of the nation's population. It is true that between 1950 and 1960 96 percent of the population growth occurred within 200 of these metropolitan areas.

While these three statements are true, they represent only part of the truth. Other parts of the whole picture are revealed by facts such as these: Between 1930 and 1968 the *urban* population of the United States increased by 110 percent, but the *rural nonfarm* population increased by 130 percent! In 1915 the number of people living in the core city was double the number living in the suburbs. The population growth of the suburbs between 1960 and 1967 was seven times greater than that of the central cities, and in 1963, for the first time, the combined population of the suburbs exceeded the total population of all of the central cities.

Between 1960 and 1965 104 metropolitan areas experienced a loss of population as a result of migration. More people moved out of these 104 metropolitan areas than moved in. While the *total* population in the metropolitan areas continued to rise, this was the result of the number of births exceeding the number of deaths by a margin large enough to more than offset this loss through migration.

A realistic appraisal of the current population picture is that while people apparently do prefer urban employment and especially an urban level of income to a rural level of income, they do *not* prefer to live in an urban environment.

Decentralization, not urbanization, is the dominant trend. This can now be documented in very persuasive terms.

Urbanized, But Not Citified!

For every two families who would prefer to live closer to the center of the urban community in which they reside, there are five families who would prefer to live farther out. This finding, from a study completed by the Institute for Social Research at the University of Michigan, is one evidence of the pressure for continued decentralization. Another is the fact that 49 percent of American people declare they would prefer to live on a farm or in a small rural village if they had complete freedom of choice. A third is that 85 percent of the families surveyed expressed a preference for a single family home. Furthermore, the higher the income level, the greater the percentage of families expressing a preference for single family housing. As family income levels rise it appears probable that many of this 49 percent who would prefer living in the country to life in the suburbs will be able to achieve their goal.

This trend also can be documented by looking at the percentage of the population living in cities with a population of 250,000 or more. In 1880, 9 percent of the total population and 31 percent of the urban population lived in large cities. By 1940 these two figures had risen to 23 and 41 percent respectively. By 1965 they had dropped to 20 and 31 percent.

Another evidence of this decentralization is the dispersion of the factories. A large proportion of the new industrial plants being constructed in this decade are being built in low density suburban and rural communities. In a three-year period in the mid-1960's one-third of all new jobs created in the United States were in counties with a population under 50,000.

PERCENTAGE OF U.S. POPULATION
LIVING IN LARGE CITIES*

Year	Of Urban Population**	Of Total Population
1840	16%	2%
1860	27	6
1880	31	9
1900	37	15
1920	40	20
1940	41	23
1950	39	23
1960	34	22
1965	31	20

* Large city is defined as city with population over 250,000.
** For reasons of consistency, the 1940 definition of urban is used.

Perhaps the major countertrend in this pattern is the growth in white-collar employment and the current trend to concentrate the sources of white-collar employment within the large central cities. Jean Gottman contends, "The modern transactional way of life depends on an increasingly larger number of white collar workers, who cannot be expected to gather where there are only one or two customers, but rather where there are thousands."

At the same time that sources of white-collar employment are being concentrated, however, the white-collar workers are seeking dispersion in their places of residence. The rise in personal income, the shortening of the work year, and the construction of freeway networks make it possible for both trends to continue.

Other Myths About Urbanism

There are a number of other myths circulating about urbanization in America that can mislead churchmen. Some have been repeated so often that they are beginning to be accepted as universal truths. Like many myths, each has an element of truth in it; but also like many myths, they can be more deceptive than helpful if used as basic assumptions in planning for the future.

Here are four illustrations of these contemporary myths about urbanism.

1. The geographical separation of place of residence and place of employment means urbanites no longer "live where they live." There is an element of truth in this, and it does apply to many business and professional men who reside in the suburbs and work in the central city. It also applies to many of the recent rural newcomers to the city. It is not true of the vast majority of urban residents. It is not true of the residents of the central city. It does not apply to the great numbers of Americans who see their job as a source of income and not as a vocation. They live where they live, not where they work.

2. The United States Supreme Court decision in *Reynolds v. Sims,* which expressed the "one man, one vote" concept, and the subsequent reapportionment of state legislatures finally gave the big cities a break in the state legislatures and in Congress.

In fact, the *Reynolds v. Sims* decision and reapportionment came too late to help the older central cities. The political advantages are accruing to the suburbs, not the central cities. The resulting "urban" legislature is largely *growth*-oriented, not *change*-centered, and therefore is of little help to the central cities.

3. The focus for urban growth in the next few decades will be the "new towns" movement. In fact, such new towns as Columbia, Reston, Clear Lake, Westlake Village, and the other 200 new towns currently on the drawing boards or under construction will accommodate no more than 10 percent of the urban growth that will occur in the United States

during the next 15 years. The 300 additional *unplanned* communities in the 25,000 to 250,000 population range will accommodate most of the increase in the urban population occurring between now and 1980.

4. We are running out of land to accommodate the urban growth of the United States. Each year between 1 and 1.5 million acres of land is converted to nonagricultural uses. In 1950 urban America occupied 18 million acres. Between 1950 and 1970 the quantity of land turned into urban uses will be larger than the acreage put into urban uses in the previous 250 years. Over one million acres of land are being covered by pavement each year, and this figure will rise to 2 million acres per year by 1985.

When one considers that (a) the land area of the United States is 1,904 million acres (exclusive of Alaska), or (b) the Census Bureau describes any enumeration district averaging 1.5 persons per acre as urbanized, it is unlikely that the United States will run out of land for urban growth before the population of the nation reaches the 6 billion mark. If the population density of the United States doubles by the year 2000, doubles again by the year 2030, and doubles again by the year 2060, it will be less than one-half that of the Netherlands in 1967.

IMPLICATIONS

The implications of this trend for the churches can only be suggested here.

One of the most obvious and already apparent implications of this trend is the difficulty metropolitan councils of city churches have in serving churches located in the outlying areas of that urban region. This problem will become more acute. Should metropolitan councils of churches be replaced by regional councils? Or should the role of state councils be enlarged?

A more subtle implication is the tendency of suburbanization to divert the suburbanite's attention (and his effective involvement) away from the large issues of the world, nation, and metropolis and to focus his attention on the issues of his municipality. This parochialism is becoming an increasingly severe problem, especially in such areas as social relations and welfare.

A third implication concerns the administrative organization of the denomination. Should the denomination be reorganized with major emphasis on relating to the people and structures of these fifteen or twenty large multi-county urban regions? Or should the emphasis be on including an urban region and its hinterland within a single judicatory? Or should the emphasis continue to be on structuring the shape of the judicatory to the size and institutional needs of the denomination?

One of the most important implications grows out of the fact that the churches already have had difficulty in relating issue-centered, specialized ministries to parishes. This decentralization trend means that this will become an even more acute problem, since most of the specialized ministries to issues and to the structures of society are found in the central city and the older nearby suburban communities.

Another important implication results from the fact that the freeways run two ways. It is relatively easy for a person working in the central city or an adjacent suburb to commute to his job from his new residence twenty or thirty miles away. It is even easier, on Sunday morning when traffic is comparatively light, to commute back in and attend worship at the church in the neighborhood where he formerly lived. Is this to be encouraged? What are the implications of the disappearance of the geographical parish?

(For some of the implications at the other end of this decentralization trend see Chapter 11.)

SUGGESTIONS FOR FURTHER READING

Bell, Daniel, et al. "Centralization and Decentralization," *Daedalus* (Summer, 1967).

Brooks, John. *The Great Leap.* New York: Harper, 1966.

Elazar, Daniel J. "Are We a Nation of Cities?" *The Public Interest* (Summer, 1966).

Wattenberg, Ben J. and Scammon, Richard M. *This U. S. A.* Rev. ed. Garden City, N. Y.: Doubleday, 1967.

2. THE INCREASE IN LEISURE: TREND OR MIRAGE?

BASIC TREND

There has been an increase in discretionary time available to Americans, but this has not resulted in an increase in leisure time.

The average number of hours worked *in a year* by the civilian population dropped from slightly over 3,300 hours in 1890 to 2,662 in 1909, to 2,205 in 1938, to 2,114 in 1950, and 1,999 in 1964. The five-day work week has become commonplace, and for many people the standard work week is now 32 to 37 hours. Out of these and similar trends has been born the myth that the United States is moving from a nation oriented to work to a society that must adjust to an increase in leisure.

A more careful look at the statistics reveals that this may be an oversimplified interpretation of cause and effect. The decrease in the number of hours worked per *year* is largely the product of two conflicting trends. One is the increase in paid time off (vacations, holidays, and sick leave). In 1967 94 percent of the persons employed in metropolitan areas received *at least* six paid holidays annually, and 97 percent of those with five or more years of service received *at least* two weeks vacation annually. An increasing proportion of the labor force now receives ten or more paid holidays and three or four weeks of paid vacation annually.

The other trend is that there have been no significant reductions in the length of the work *week* since 1950, and in recent years the length of the work week has actually increased for many individuals. Between 1960 and 1966, for example, the length of the work week increased by an average of two hours for persons employed in mining, manufacturing, and construction.

The net result of these two trends is that while the number of weeks (and days) worked per year has dropped sharply because of the increase in paid time off for vacations and holidays, the number of hours worked *per year* has declined only slightly in recent years because of the increase in the length of the average work week.

A much more important change in this matter of work and leisure has been the reduction in the number of years the average American spends as an active member of the labor force. In the United States in 1963 only 36 percent of the persons in the 15-19 age group were active members of the labor force. In West Germany, Switzerland, and the United Kingdom this figure ranged from 66 to 73 percent. The typical American male spends five years less than his European counterpart as an active member of the labor force.

A comparison of today and yesterday in the United States shows the same pattern. The age at which individuals enter the labor force is rising, and the age of retirement from the labor market is dropping. In March 1966 there were only

2 million men age 65 and over in the labor force—the lowest such total since 1940. During this 26-year period the number of men age 65 and over doubled.

In 1900 62 percent of all males age 14 to 19 and 63.1 percent of all males age 65 and over were in the labor force. By 1955 these figures had dropped to 49 percent and 38.5 percent respectively, and by 1965 were down to 43.8 percent and 26.9 percent. These figures are expected to decline to 35 percent and 22 percent respectively by 1980.

An examination of how Americans spend their time reveals several other trends that are relevant to this discussion of leisure: (1) As a result of the opportunities to increase his income in 1967 the average employed American worked five and one-half days, or 46 hours a week; (2) 3.6 million persons with full-time employment also held a second job, up 20 percent since 1960, and averaged 13 hours a week as moonlighters; (3) there were over 17 million wives employed outside the home, compared to 9 million in 1950 and only 5 million in 1940; (4) in 1940 only 9 percent of the mothers with children under 18 years of age were employed outside the home, and by 1965 this figure had jumped to 35 percent; (5) the proportion of the labor force employed as professionals, executives, and technicians doubled between 1951 and 1968—and the typical executive or professional person worked between 50 and 65 hours a week; and (6) the journey from home to work took about 30 percent more time than it did 30 years ago.

Clearly what has happened is that Americans have had the opportunity for an increase in their leisure time, but have rejected this in favor of an increase in income. As John K. Galbraith has pointed out, in the old industrial society "toil was dreary, repetitive and physically painful." Fifty years ago the 84-hour work week was the standard for millions of men. In the new industrial state work is more likely to be pleasant, even fascinating. Today instead of working to survive, the employee works to be able to satisfy a constantly expanding list of wants. Given this changed set of circumstances the typical American is more likely to choose more work rather than more leisure.

Considerable evidence can be assembled to support this contention that the typical American prefers work and its rewards to leisure and its rewards. This can be illustrated by the 10 million housewives with young children at home who have entered the labor force in recent years, or by the fact that a decrease in the length of the work week for men results in an increase in the number who go out and secure a second job. It can be illustrated by the hundreds of thousands of young people who drop out of school to take a full-time job, or by the fact that one person out of six refuses his vacation each year.

It also can be illustrated by the choices Americans make when confronted with the alternative of more money or more leisure. Rarely is the decision made to choose leisure. A few years ago the United Steel Workers union bargained successfully for a 13-week sabbatical for employees every five years. In those plants where the employees had a choice the majority traded their sabbatical for a savings plan. In one of the plants of the Armco Steel Corporation 80 percent of the salaried workers chose to increase their financial compensation by working all 13 weeks.

This same distaste for leisure was revealed by a recent study of men drawing benefits under Social Security. When asked why they retired only 17 percent replied that they retired in good health in order to enjoy leisure. Most of them retired either because of the employer's decision that they should retire (39 percent) or because of poor health (35 percent). Many of those who retired to enjoy more free time subsequently went back to work, and two out of three of all retired men in good health went back to a full-time job for at least six months after their initial retirement. Most of those in good health who did not have a post-retirement job explained that this was because they could not find employment, not because they preferred leisure to work.

Economists have calculated that during the first half of this century the benefits to workers from the increase in productivity were divided into two categories. One-third of this increase was used to increase the time free of work (earlier retirement, later entry into the labor force, a shorter work week, and more paid vacation and holidays), and two-thirds was directed to an increase in income. During the first third of the second half of this century an even greater emphasis in allocating the proceeds of increased productivity has been on increasing the buying power of the worker through higher wages, larger salaries, and bigger pensions.

The only recent significant move to allocate the fruits of greater productivity to an increase in leisure has been the trend toward earlier retirement. (In 1968 one half of all persons applying for Social Security benefits for the first time were sixty-two years of age.) As was pointed out earlier, however, most men who retire do so involuntarily and not out of a desire for free time. It appears that in the United States the major consideration in establishing old-age benefits and in lowering the age of retirement has been to reduce the number of persons in the labor market rather than as a response to a national demand for more leisure. The best recent example of this was the pension program negotiated by United Automobile Workers that enabled a worker with 30 years of service to retire at 55 with a pension of $250 a month. This was openly presented as a means of removing the excess labor from an industry where automation is producing a rapid increase in the average productivity per worker.

The data presented thus far strongly suggest that many deceptive myths have grown up around this subject of discretionary time and leisure. Another means of testing this is to look at how people actually do spend their time. During the past four decades social scientists have developed the concept of the "time budget" and have used this technique to discover how people actually spend each minute in a 24-hour day.

A comparison of four of these time budget studies (the Multination Time-Budget Research Project reported in 1966; G. Lundberg *et al., Leisure: A Suburban Study,* 1934; Sorokin and Berger, *Time-Budgets of Human Behavior,* 1939; and the 1954 J. A. Ward-Mutual Broadcasting Company study) suggests that the major source of additional potential leisure for Americans during the past two or three decades has been that sleeping time has been reduced by nearly an hour. Other changes suggested by a comparison of these studies are (1) an increase in the time spent away from home, (2) an increase in hours worked (all jobs) each week, (3) an increase in time spent traveling, (4) an increase in time spent on housework and care of children by housewives, (5) an increase in time spent shopping, (6) a decrease in time spent eating, (7) a decrease in time spent visiting, (8) a 50 percent decrease in time spent reading, (9) an increase in time spent watching television, (10) *in summary, a decrease in leisure* time of over an hour a day.

IMPLICATIONS

Perhaps the most pressing issue raised for the churches by this increase in discretionary time is a doctrinal question that concerns the nature of men. What are the theological and moral implications of this pattern which sees the typical American voluntarily choosing a larger income rather than more leisure? The larger income often is not necessary for survival or personal security. In fact, it frequently is used largely to increase the worker's capacity to purchase luxuries. Is this choice a result of society's mores, which make hard work, a larger income, and an increase in material prosperity an object of esteem?

Closely related are the moral implications of the recent trend that makes the older worker the object of efforts to reduce the supply of labor. Lowering the age of mandatory retirement is one means of reducing the supply of available labor. But is it morally right to do this? Or should this goal be achieved by a combination of alternatives that would include reducing the length of the work week, increasing the length of vacations, and developing more extensive retraining programs?

An examination of the reactions of people to the opportunity for increased free time and more leisure strongly suggests there is widespread resistance to this. People prefer to be employed. Should there be a national policy that requires a broader distribution of the increasing amount of free time that will be available to the adult population? Instead of forcing older persons to accept a disproportionately large share of this free time through mandatory early retirement, should this "burden" be shared by younger persons? Or should housewives be discouraged from entering the labor force? (While many of the conditions are different, there is a parallel between these questions and those raised during the Great Depression of 1929-1941 when the problem was also one of an excess of labor and a shortage of jobs.)

The gradual diminution of the need for a large labor supply means that fewer people will be employed or a larger number of people will be employed for fewer years. When this has occurred in the past in the United States it has produced unemployment and the dole. Is the current emphasis on leisure an attempt to avoid the use of these two unpleasant words? Or is it possible to develop a doctrine of leisure that supplements the traditional Puritan work ethic? Can this be done within the context of the Christian doctrine of man? Thus far, forced free time and the weakening of the work ethic has tended to produce disaffection, disenchantment, rebellion, and hedonism.

Galbraith argues for wider options for the employed person than is now available. He contends the standard work week is a poor unit to use as the base for arranging free time. Should the 15- or 20-hour work week become the standard? This would make it easier for the person who preferred leisure to work to earn a minimum living and still leave those who prefer work to leisure to work a 45- to 60-hour week.

In addition to these general philosophical questions that concern society as a whole and to which the churches should respond, this increase in discretionary time also raises specific questions for the local church.

When this matter of increased leisure first arose the typical response was centered on the need to keep people busy. One result was the creation of hundreds of "golden age clubs." The emphasis usually was on arts, crafts, lectures, and fellowship. More recently has come the recognition that the primary need of the person with a larger amount of free time is not simply to be busy, but rather to be busy in a meaningful manner. This is especially important for the man who has built his life around work and then is arbitrarily forced to retire.

As this is more widely recognized, and as the number of individuals with a surplus of free time increases, it means that the parish seeking to minister to these people is faced with challenges and opportunities that are more complex than they formerly appeared. Instead of planning programs *for* older people that will occupy their time and fill up the hours in a lonely day, the new call is to help these individuals find new and meaningful roles in life. One of the most creative responses in this direction is in those parishes which invite persons with free time to share in carrying out the ministry of the church. Instead of viewing these persons as an object of ministry, they are asked to become partners in ministry. One of the implications of this is that both laymen and clergy must come to view the parish, not the seminary, as the basic training ground for ministry.

One of the most common responses by pastors to the contemporary folklore about leisure is the comment, "If everyone has so much leisure time, how come our church has so much difficulty in recruiting volunteer leaders?" Such a question implies that perhaps the widespread discussion about the increase in leisure is a myth. This question also reflects the common tendency of parishes to overwork the overworked and ignore the idle. This is consistent with the normal institutional pressures that place the highest priority on getting the job done and a much lower priority on making sure it is a rewarding experience for the person who is given the responsibility.

The parish that is looking for participants and volunteers from among those who have experienced an increase in free time should recognize (1) that the increase in actual leisure time has been limited to a relatively few segments of the population; (2) that while many people in the 25 to 60 age range are open and receptive to meaningful new experiences, relatively few are simply looking for something to fill up a bloc of leisure time; and (3) that many elderly people are unsure of their ability to successfully complete a strange new task, and the fear of failure is a major problem for most people of all ages.

Local churches also would be well advised to recognize that they do not stand alone in responding to the conditions created by an increase in the discretionary time available to many people. Frequently they can be most helpful by participating as part of a joint effort. An excellent example can be found by looking at how literally millions of housewives and mothers have responded to an increase in discretionary time. Some have gone into the labor market and secured full-time jobs. Over one-half of the women age 45 to 54 are employed outside the home. Others are going back to college in rapidly rising numbers. In 1964, for example, 90,000 women in the 30-34 age bracket were enrolled in colleges and universities. A year later this figure had jumped nearly 30 percent to 115,000! Hundreds of thousands of others have found meaningful roles as volunteers in hospitals, schools, social agencies, political parties, and other organizations.

This suggests that in each community one or two local churches might specialize in helping those persons with an excess of discretionary time to become aware of the variety of opportunities that are available to them. In some communities this might mean the churches should assist in broadening the range of such opportunities.

SUGGESTIONS FOR FURTHER READING

American Behavioral Scientist, December, 1966. (This issue contains the details of and a series of articles on the Multination Time-Budget Research Project.)

Brightbill, Charles K. *The Challenge of Leisure*. Englewood Cliffs, N.J.: Prentice-Hall, 1963.

DeGrazia, Sebastian. *Of Time, Work and Leisure*. Garden City, N.Y.: Doubleday, 1962.

Galbraith, John Kenneth. *The New Industrial State*. Boston: Houghton Mifflin, 1967.

Kreps, Juanita M. *Lifetime Allocation of Work and Leisure*. Social Security Administration, U. S. Department of Health, Education, and Welfare, 1968.

Lee, Robert. *Religion and Leisure in America*. Nashville: Abingdon Press, 1964.

Main, Jeremy. "Good Living Begins at $25,000 a Year," *Fortune* (May, 1968).

Robinson, John P. "Social Change as Measured by Time-Budgets." Survey Research Center, the University of Michigan, 1967.

Wentworth, Edna C. *Employment After Retirement*. Social Security Administration, the U. S. Department of Health, Education, and Welfare, 1968.

3. THE CHANGING SHAPE OF THE FAMILY

BASIC TREND

The nature and characteristics of the American family are changing.

An impressive array of evidence can be assembled to support the contention that the family is being subjected to unprecedented changes that will drastically alter both the form and the function of the family in American society.

Anthropologist Margaret Mead has suggested that the family will change radically by the year 2000 when "a new style with an emphasis on very small families" will free most of the people in the U. S. to function primarily as individuals rather than as family members.

Robert S. Morison, Director of Cornell University's Division of Biological Sciences, contends the American family will continue to suffer a decline in prestige primarily

42

because it no longer can transmit the new knowledge required for survival in a rapidly changing world.

The family is being "de-tribalized." The number of one-generation and one-person households is increasing rapidly. The proportions of households including three or four generations is decreasing. The average size of American households dropped from 5.79 persons per household in 1790 to 5.04 persons in 1800 to 4.93 persons in 1890 to 4.11 persons in 1930 to 3.38 persons in 1960 to 3.28 in 1967. One often overlooked reason for this is the gradual disappearance of the maiden aunt from the home of her brother or sister.

The number of households composed of unrelated individuals (about 65 percent are one-person households) now has passed the 13 million level. The number of one-person households is increasing three times as rapidly as the increase in households composed of families. (The number of one-person households increased from 4 million in 1950 to 7 million in 1960 to nearly 10 million in 1968.)

Divorce has become a common element of the family picture, as one out of five marriages ends in divorce (but not two out of five or one out of three as is often alleged by those who misinterpret the statistics on divorce).

One-sixth of all married persons are now living with their second (or third or fourth or fifth) marriage partner.

It would be easy to enlarge this list to underscore the point that the family ties are becoming looser, and the strains being placed on the family are becoming greater.

It is not the purpose of this book, however, to reinforce a stereotype that may be more misleading than it is helpful. The objective here is to highlight a few national trends that are affecting the family, to destroy some of the more common myths about the American family, and to suggest why the churches should be interested in these trends.

The Typical Family

The typical American family has changed substantially, but despite the cries of the alarmists most of the changes are for the better! An increasing number and proportion of the American people apparently *prefer* living within rather than outside the family.

A larger proportion of the adult population is married, marriages last longer than formerly, married people live longer, and the number of childless marriages is decreasing. In other words Americans appear to be voting in favor of marriage and the family. (For another endorsement of marriage see Proverbs 18:22, "He who finds a wife finds a good thing, and obtains favor from the Lord.") The typical family has fewer relatives living with it, it has fewer deaths among the members living at home, and it has a higher income than ever before in history.

These generalizations can be translated into specific statements that suggest the family is not about to disintegrate. In 1890 in the typical family either the husband or wife usually died before the youngest child was married. The average wife found herself widowed after 33 years of married life. In 1968 the typical widow had been married for 44 years before her husband died. The average widower back in 1890 found his marriage dissolved by the death of his wife 31 years after their wedding day; in 1968 this had gone up to 43 years.

The childless marriage is also disappearing. Given a greater freedom of choice married adults apparently prefer being parents to being childless. In 1950 20 percent of the women in the 45 to 49 age group who had ever been married were childless. By 1965 this figure had dropped to 14 percent, and by 1975 it is expected that only 9 percent of the married women in the 45-49 age group will be childless.

Likewise the number of families with only one child dropped by a fourth during the 1950's.

While the number of childless families is dropping, the orphan is rapidly disappearing from the American scene. As recently as 1920 one child out of six under the age of 18 had lost one or both parents, and there were 750,000 children who had lost both parents. By 1965, despite the fact that the child population had nearly doubled, there were only 70,000 children who had lost both parents, and the proportion who had lost one parent dropped from 14.4 percent in 1920 to 4.6 percent.

The maiden aunt and the bachelor uncle also are disappearing as an ever greater percentage of adults choose the married state. In 1940 10 percent of the women in the 25-44 age bracket were single. By 1965 that figure had been cut in half as only 5 percent were single, and it is expected to drop to 3 percent by 1980. The percentage of those who were married and living with their husbands rose from 81 percent to 88 percent in this quarter century period. If people today shied away from marriage to the same extent they did in the 1930's there would be an additional 3 million spinsters age 35 and over in the population (and of course that would mean there also would be 3 million more bachelors on the loose). Population experts are now predicting that 96 percent of today's boys and girls will marry.

Family incomes have been rising at an unprecedented rate. In the 21 years from 1929 to 1950 the average (mean) family income, after allowing for the impact of inflation, rose by less than 25 percent or about one percent per year. In the 18-year period from 1950 to 1968, again using constant dollars to offset the impact of inflation, the average family income rose over 50 percent, or an average of 2.5 percent per year compounded annually. In 1950 only 300,000 individuals or couples had a taxable income of $25,000 or more. In 1968 there were 1,500,000 or nearly five times as many in that bracket.

Likewise the typical family today has more privacy than was the case a generation or two ago. In 1947 2.3 million married couples were sharing living quarters with relatives. This was 7 percent of all married couples compared to 5.6 percent in 1910 and 5.4 percent in 1940. By 1968, however, this proportion had dropped to 1.6 percent. These figures support the contention that the three-generation household of yesterday was a matter not of choice, but rather of necessity.

Elderly people apparently are adjusting to the disappearance of the three-generation household. In early 1968 seven out of eight men age 65 and over were the heads of their own households, three out of four women in that age group either were the wives of the heads of a separate family or serving as the heads of their own households. Apparently most older men and women both prefer and are able to maintain their own homes. Studies made of housing for the elderly indicate that older persons greatly prefer to maintain their own homes as long as they possibly can.

In 1947 seven out of eight families (87.2 percent to be exact) were headed by a husband-wife team. Twenty years later seven out of eight families (87.2 percent to be exact) were headed by a husband-wife team. The projections of the Bureau of the Census indicate that in 1985 seven out of eight (87.4 percent to be exact) of all families will be headed by a husband-wife team. (The reference here is to families, not households. Only 73 percent of all *households* are headed by a husband-wife team.) This suggests that contrary to the predictions of Miss Mead and others the family may not be in a state of rapid disintegration. It is hard to believe that in the 30 years between 1970 and 2000 the form of the family will drastically change.

Despite the pessimistic view of the family expressed by a number of futurists, the American people are displaying a growing preference for married life and for a family with two or more children.

There are, however, four other trends that are having an impact on many families, that indicate a sharp change from the past, and that should be of special interest to churchmen concerned about the ministry of tomorrow's church.

The first is the rise in marriages across religious lines. A review of the studies on this subject indicates that (1) the rates of intermarriage are rising and will continue to climb—in some parts of the nation nearly one half of the Protestants and Catholics now marry outside their faith, while for the nation as a whole about one out of every six Jews marries someone who is not Jewish, (2) marriages across religious lines are more likely to end in divorce or separation than marriages where both partners are of the same faith, and (3) when the mother and father come from different religious heritages this difference often is a source of conflict in rearing the children.

The second trend is that the family is gaining a greater degree of freedom and being confronted with more tension-producing choices as the amount of the family income climbs and the amount of discretionary time also increases. The decisions on how to dispose of these two "surpluses" is potentially one of the greatest sources of increased happiness—or increased tension—in the family of tomorrow.

A third source of concern is the sharp rise in illegitimate births. According to the reports of the National Center for Health Statistics the number of illegitimate births tripled in the 25-year period from 1940 to 1965. In 1940 there were seven illegitimate births for every 1000 unmarried women in the 15-44 age group. In 1965 this figure was up to 23 per 1000. In 1940 90,000 illegitimate births were recorded; in the next 15 years the total doubled to 183,000; and jumped to 302,400 in 1966. What is perhaps a better index—the illegitimacy ratio—reveals the same trend, but a less rapid rise. In 1940 38 out of every 1000 births were illegitimate. In 1967 84 births out of 1,000 (or 8.4 percent) were illegitimate. While the total number of births has been decreasing, the number of illegitimate births has been rising. In Akron, Ohio, for example, between 1952 and 1965 the total number of births dropped from 7,147 to 4,933, but during the same period of time the number of illegitimate births rose from 280 to 619.

Between 1955 and 1965 the number of illegitimate births among nonwhite women increased by 40 percent; among white women it rose by 93 percent.

Furthermore, the number of babies born in wedlock but conceived before marriage is rising. In 1945 8 percent of the white brides gave birth to a baby within eight months after being married; in 1965 this figure was up to 16 percent. (For nonwhite brides it was about 40 percent in both years.)

The fourth disturbing trend concerns the number of families headed by a woman with no husband present. It is comforting to point out that 90 percent of the families with children under 18 years of age are headed by a husband-wife team. A look at the other 10 percent reveals that nine out of ten are headed by a woman with no husband present. Furthermore a disproportionately high percentage are Negro families. While only 8 percent of the white families with children under 18 are one-parent families, 28 percent of all Negro families are headed by a father or mother without the spouse being present in the home. This is a part of the problem described by Daniel P. Moynihan in the highly controversial "Moynihan Report" on the Negro family. (See Suggestions for Further Reading at the end of Chapter 6.)

Divorce and Separation

Divorce figures often are used to support the contention that the family structure is not as strong as formerly.

The statistics on divorces lend themselves to misinterpretation and to alarming prophecies about the future. It must be remembered that the divorce rate peaked in 1946 at 17.8 divorces per 1,000 married women and dropped to 10.1 in 1952. Since 1953 the divorce rate has remained remarkably steady and hovered around the 9.5 to 10.5 figure. This is not as high as some alarmists suggest, since the divorce rate during the years immediately preceding World War II ranged from 8.3 in 1936 to 9.4 in 1941. In 1920 the rate was 8.0 divorces per 1,000 married women.

One of the most important recent changes in the pattern of divorces is the duration of the marriage before it ends in divorce. In 1950 the median duration of marriage for persons receiving a divorce or annulment was 5.3 years. Six years later the figure was up to 6.4 years, and in 1965 it had climbed to 7.2 years. This suggests that more long-term marriages are terminating in divorce. Perhaps this means more couples now feel economically and psychologically free to choose divorce rather than to perpetuate an unsatisfactory marriage.

One-sixth of all married persons are now living in their second (or subsequent) marriage. The median age for remarriage has climbed to 40.2 years for men and 35.6 years for women. In 1964 slightly over one-fourth of the brides had been married at least once previously. Three-fourths of these women taking the marriage vows for the second (or third or fourth) time were divorcées, and one-fourth were widows. It should be noted, however, that of all divorcées 96 percent have been divorced only once.

Approximately 80 percent of all divorced men and 71

percent of all divorced women remarry—and three times out of five marry another divorced person.

In 1962 two out of five divorces occurred in marriages in which there were no children under age 18. In another 23 percent the couple had only one child, while only 18 percent of the divorces were in families with three or more children.

In 1940 only 1.4 percent of the adult population was currently divorced. By 1965 this figure had risen to 2.6 percent —owing in part to the increased popularity of marriage mentioned earlier, in part to the increase in life expectancy, and in part to the fact that about one-fourth of the persons who sought a divorce back in the 1946-52 era when the divorce rate was so high never remarried.

The number of divorces, the divorce rate (per 1,000 married women), and the number of divorced people is certain to rise during the next 15 years. This should be anticipated, and it should be understood that this rise will be primarily a result of the fact that the number of marriages will rise sharply. Since most divorces occur during the first years of marriage this increase in the number of marriages will produce a similar increase in the number of divorces *and* a disproportionately high increase in the divorce rate. A doubling of the number of marriages probably will be accompanied by a subsequent doubling of the number of divorces. In 1960 there were nearly 400,000 divorces involving nearly 800,000 adults. By 1967 the number had risen to 500,000, and it probably will reach the 800,000 level by 1975 or 1980.

On the other hand it should be remembered that in 1967 out of every 1,000 married men only 31 currently were divorced, 20 were separated from their wives, 48 were widowed, and 900 were living with their wives. (Perhaps of greater significance is the fact that out of every 1,000 married white males 13 were separated from their wives and 30 were divorced, while out of every 1,000 married nonwhite males 87 were separated and 45 were divorced.)

On the feminine side of the family, in 1967 there were 58 million women in the country who had ever been married (compared to only 49 million men who had ever been married and were still alive to tell the story to the census taker). Out of these 58 million women over 9 million (16 percent, or 160 out of every 1,000) were widows, two and a third million were currently divorced (4 percent, or 40 out of every 1,000), slightly over 1.5 million (3 percent, or 30 out of every 1,000) were legally separated from their husbands, and 43 million (75 percent, or 750 out of every 1,000) were living with their husbands. In other words, death is four times more likely to break up a woman's marriage than is divorce.

Changing Role of the Housewife

One of the greatest changes in family life is in the old pattern of the husband and father going out in the world to earn a living for the family while the mother remained at home to take care of the house and children. In 1940 there were 6.7 million *single* women in the labor force. By 1967 this number had dropped to 6.0 million. During the same period the number of *married* women in the labor force rose from 5 million to 17.5 million. In 1940 only 9 percent of the mothers with children under the age of 18 were employed outside the home. By March, 1966 this figure had climbed to 35 percent. In early 1967 two out of every five women in the labor force had children under 18 years old, and the number of working wives rose from 8.6 million in 1950 (48 percent of the female labor force) to 15.9 million in 1967 (59 percent of the female labor force). Married women accounted for nearly one-half of the increase in the labor force between 1960 and 1966. Perhaps the most significant factor in attempting to project the future direction of this trend can be seen by noting that (1) the level of education of women is rising (see Chapter 9), (2) the higher her husband's income, the less likely the wife is to be engaged in paid employment, and (3) the more schooling a mother has had, the more likely she is to be employed outside the home. (Only 43 percent of the housewives with only an elementary school education were employed outside the home compared to 53 percent of those with a high school diploma, 68 percent of those with a college degree, and 81 percent of those with a degree from a graduate school.) The sum of these forces, plus the inevitable increase in the number of married women, forms the basis for the prediction by the Department of Labor that during the 1970's there will be a 43 percent increase in the number of working mothers with children under the age of six.

In pre-World War II days the parents in middle-class families shared a joint responsibility for bringing up the children. This has changed. The Harvard Class of 1939 was surveyed 25 years after graduation (1964), and 6 percent of the fathers responding said the primary problem in handling their children was the issue of moral values; 78 percent said their main worry was earning the money to pay for raising the children.

The Impact of Urbanization

Sometimes the fact that the divorce rate among urban residents is twice as high as among farm families is cited to support the argument that urbanization is having as adverse effect on the family.

There is a growing body of expert opinion, however, that contends that urbanization strengthens the family. Proponents of this view contend that in an urban society the family becomes the natural place for discussing and solving difficult problems and making complex choices. They add that the urban scene provides more educational and economic opportunities, and these tend to strengthen the family by reducing economic tensions. An urban society produces fewer bachelors and spinsters. A variety of studies have indicated that relatives still make up an important element in the life of the urban family, and sometimes kinship ties are strengthened by urbanization.

The disappearance of employment opportunities in rural areas has meant that members of the family either have to leave home or travel an unusually long distance in order to find a job. By contrast in the urban community the place of work and the place of residence may be closely related.

Finally, it should be emphasized that the most important source of tension and conflict in the family is not the proximity of relatives nor the degree of urbanization of the environment. The most important source of tension in a marriage is the degree of economic success of the husband. Several studies have revealed very clearly that the wife's affection for her husband was influenced more by the husband's economic ups and downs than by any other factor. Since poverty is relatively more common in rural communities than in urban areas and since the bulk of the current efforts to eliminate poverty is devoted to the urban scene, it may be argued that urbanization improves the stability of the family.

IMPLICATIONS

Some of the implications of these facts and trends for the churches are more obvious than others.

Perhaps the most obvious implication is that those who argue that the family-oriented church is obsolete are standing on shaky ground. Currently over 92 percent of all the people in the United States are living in a family environment, despite the increased social and economic freedom that enables more people than ever before to maintain separate households. The changing age mix of the population and the increase in affluence indicate that this figure will drop to perhaps 86 or 87 percent by 1980, but even that means that seven out of every eight persons will be a part of a functioning family unit.

An even more important implication, however, is the challenge to the churches to take a new look at their value systems in the light of the findings of recent research on the family. For example, many churchmen believe that for the mother to be employed outside the home has an adverse effect on the family. However, research by Robert O. Blood, Eleanor Maccaby, and others suggests that the mother's employment outside the home is not harmful either to the family structure or to the children. Since the tensions produced by an inadequate income are destructive to family life, it would be better for the churches to strive to increase employment opportunities rather than to support the continuation of a welfare system that forces many mothers to stay home and try to maintain a family on an inadequate income.

Likewise the churches may want to reassess their traditional stand on divorce. Again recent research indicates that people seeking a divorce are not sinners who simply want to trade in an old playmate for a new one, but rather are persons who are extremely eager to have a happy family life.

Since the local church is usually viewed as a strong supporter of the family (and recently has been widely criticized for this strong family orientation), and since nine out of ten Americans are living in a family arrangement, the churches would be well advised to mobilize the resources and develop the skills that would enable them to help families counter the forces that tend to destroy family life.

There are several dimensions to this. The increase in the

two-generation family and the rapid decline of the extended family mean that the responsibility for raising children, once shared informally among several relatives, is now largely the responsibility of one or two adults. The churches must recognize and respond to this heavier strain now being placed on parents.

In the same vein there is an increasing openness on the part of the various members of the family to receive help in discovering and more effectively fulfilling their roles as family members. There also is an increasing understanding on the part of all the major denominations of this need. As a result the denominations are providing the tools to help the local church in this phase of its ministry—preparation for marriage, sex education, and continuing opportunities for people to increase their understanding of the demands on them as spouses or as parents. One result is that the local church often is the weakest link in bringing together these needs and resources.

Another implication of this same development is that the educational approach to family life is beginning to gain greater prominence in contrast to the counseling-after-problems-arise approach that has dominated the churches' ministry in this area.

On the other hand, while the vast majority of people are living in a family environment, the changing age mixture of the population, the increase in the economic resources of young single persons, and the rapidly increasing number of widows means that the churches also must give serious thought to how they minister to non-family persons.

In more specific terms, the churches should be thinking of how they can reach, serve, and minister to specific target groups of the population. These include the 10 million working mothers with children under 18 years of age, the 19 million married couples who are not in the child-rearing phase of the family cycle, the 13 million adults living in separate households outside the family structure, the estimated 3 million preschool children who are growing up in homes that do not provide the environment necessary to start them off on an equal footing when they enter school, the 2.5 million mothers with children under the age of 18 but with no man in the house (together they have 5.8 million children), the 300,000 women who gave birth to an illegitimate child last year, the uncounted number of couples who married across faith lines, and the 4 million currently divorced persons.

The local church that looks at the people in its parish in these terms may be stimulated to think of new ways to minister to people, both inside and outside the family. The parish that assumes this attitude will affect the future and the shape of the family in America in 1985. Perhaps the most important variable in predicting the future of the family is the attitude and creativity of the local church. By its actions and inactions it will help determine the future of the family in the United States.

SUGGESTIONS FOR FURTHER READING

Bell, Norman W. and Vogel, Ezra F., *A Modern Introduction to the Family*. New York: The Free Press, 1960.

Blood, Robert O. and Wolfe, Donald. *Husbands and Wives.* New York: Free Press, 1962.

Bronfenbrenner, Urie. "The Split-Level American Family," *Saturday Review* (October 7, 1967).

Denton, Wallace. *What's Happening to Our Families?* Philadelphia: Westminster Press, 1963.

Fairchild, Roy W. and Wynn, John Charles. *Families in the Church*. New York: Association Press, 1961.

Kenkel, William F. *The Family in Perspective.* New York: Appleton-Century-Crofts, 1966.

Komarovsky, Mirra. *Blue-Collar Marriage.* New York: Vintage Books, 1967.

Mead, Margaret. "The Life Cycle and Its Variations: The Division of Roles." *Daedalus* (Summer, 1967).

Peterson, Esther. "Working Women." *Daedalus* (Spring, 1964).

Sanna, Victor. *Marriage Counseling: Psychology-Ideology.* Springfield, Ill.: Charles Thomas, 1968.

Uthe, Edward W. (ed.). *Social Change: An Assessment of Current Trends.* Philadelphia: Fortress Press, 1968.

4. THE GENERATION GAP

BASIC TREND

The age mix of the American population will change as the number and proportion of younger and of older persons increases while the number of those in the 35 to 45 age bracket decreases in both absolute and comparative terms.

Recently it has become fashionable to point dramatically to the fact that by 1975 one-half of the residents of the United States will not yet have reached their twenty-fifth birthday. This is an important point for at least two reasons. First it is not true. In 1975 the median age of the population will be about 27 years—down slightly, if at all, from the 1969 median of 27.3 years. Second, it should be remembered that in 1880 the median age of the American population was 20.9 years, and as late as 1930 it was 26.5 years. In 1950 it was 30.2 years, and in 1960 the median was 29.5 years. The projections of the Bureau of the Census indicate that in 1985 the median age of the American people will be between 25.6 and 29.4 years—and probably will be close to 27.5 years.

Out of this myth that young people soon will dominate the American scene to an unprecedented extent has come the phrase, "the generation gap." There is no question but that there is a communication problem between young people in the 15 to 25 age bracket and the generation over 40 years of age. It also is possible that this may be a greater gap and more difficult to bridge than ever before.

There is another generation gap, however, that can be described in more objective terms and that constitutes one of the important developments of this half of the twentieth century.

This is the gap in the size of the generations produced by fluctuations in the birth rate. There are two gaps in the chart or diagram illustrating the age distribution of the American population. The first gap refers to those persons born in the 1928-1941 period when the number of babies born each year dropped well below the 2.8 million annual average that prevailed before and after that 14 year period. The second gap is a result of the decline in the number of births that began in 1957 and continued through the 1960's. The number of babies born in 1967 was 700,000 less than the number born a decade earlier.

As time passes these two sharp drops in the number of births are reflected in any description of the age distribution of the population. Persons born before or after these two gaps are more numerous than those who were born in either of these two periods of history.

The changes in the age distribution of the population have produced a variety of problems and responses. When cereal manufacturers saw what the decline in births in the early 1960's was going to do to their sales they began placing a much greater emphasis in their advertising on reaching teen-agers and elderly persons.

When the boom in marriages that was expected to begin in the mid 1960's (20 years after the baby boom that began in 1945) did not materialize, the demographers went back to check their statistics. They found, as they expected, that there were plenty of young ladies in the 18-21 age bracket to produce a marriage boom, but they also were reminded that the typical bridegroom is two to three years older than his bride. Because of this difference in the age at marriage the number of women in the "marrying age" group (age 18-21) was nearly 600,000 larger than the number of men in the appropriate age bracket (age 20-23). This di-lemma, sometimes referred to as the "marriage squeeze" was a temporary phenomenon and soon disappeared. In 1965 there were 76 21-year-old men (the most common age for the bridegroom) for every 100 18-year-old women (the most common age for brides). But in 1968 there were 110 21-year-old men for every 100 18-year-old women, and everyone—including several hundred anxious mothers—was happy again.

In the late 1967 and early 1968 when people began look-ing to the forthcoming presidential election campaign many political pundits suggested that the election might be decided by the votes of the young people. They noted that the num-ber of persons in the under-age-35 group numbered over 35 million—a substantial bloc.

They overlooked three important considerations, how-ever. First, the number of persons in the age 50 and over group was much larger—nearly 50 million Americans have passed their fiftieth birthday—than the under-age-35 group. (In 1985, however, the under-age-35 group will outnumber the over-age-50 group by about 57 million to 56 million.) Second, older people vote with greater regularity than young persons. In the 1966 elections 61 percent of the members of the "fifty-fifty club" (the nearly 50 million persons age 50 and over) cast their ballots, compared to less than 41 percent of the members of the "thirty-five thirty-five club." At the extremes 47 percent of the persons age 75 and over voted in the 1966 elections, compared to only 32 percent of those age 21 to 24. A similar pattern prevailed in 1968.

In the emotionally charged presidential election of 1964 51 percent of those age 21-24 voted compared to 72 percent of those age 50 and over and 65 percent of those 25 to 34 years of age. In that same election 71 percent of the whites voted compared to 59 percent of the Negroes of voting age. In 1968, 69 percent of all whites old enough to vote cast a ballot, compared to 56 percent of the nonwhites.

A third factor worth noting on this point is that the public opinion polls have revealed that the vast majority of young people voting for the first time choose the same party and the same candidates as their parents.

Before looking at the implications for the churches of the changing age distribution of the population, it may be helpful to review some of the more important changes.

1. *An increase in the number of older persons.* The number of Americans who have passed their sixty-fifth birthday is rising at an average rate of nearly 1,000 per day during the 1960's, and this pace will continue during the entire 1965-85 period. The number of these senior citizens will increase from 18 million in 1965 to 25 million in 1985. However they will constitute a decreasing proportion of the total population. In 1965 one person out of every 11 had passed his sixty-fifth birthday. In 1985 this proportion will be one out of 12.

2. *An increase in the number of pre-retirement older persons.* The number of persons in the 55-64 age group has been increasing, and is expected to increase through 1985. (During the 1985-95 period, however, there will be a decrease

in the size of this age group.) During this 20-year period the number of persons in this pre-retirement age range will increase from 17 million in 1965 to 21.2 million in 1985—an increase substantially less than that occurring in the over 65 age group. In 1960 the latter group exceeded the 55-64 age group by one million persons, in 1985 the difference will be nearly four million persons.

3. *A slight decrease and later a sharp increase in the number of persons age 35-54.* Between 1965 and 1975 the number of Americans in the 35 to 54 age group will decrease from 46.5 million to 46 million. This number will rise slightly to 47.5 million in 1980 and then shoot up to 52.8 million in 1985. (In 1990 this age group will total 61 million persons and be up to 69 million in 1995.)

4. *A sharp increase in the 20 to 34 age group.* During this 20-year period the number of Americans in the 20-34 age group will rise sharply—from 36 million in 1965 to 61.7 million in 1985. In 1968, for example, the number of persons celebrating their twenty-second birthday was 2.8 million. A year later that number jumped to 3.8 million—and one result was an increase in seminary enrollment.

It should be remembered that this 20-34 age group not only accounts for nearly nine out of every ten students in seminary, this age group also produces four out of five babies born each year. The number of persons in this age group will increase by 70 percent between 1965 and 1985.

5. *A modest increase in the number of persons in the 10-19 age group.* This is a more speculative projection than the first four since most of the persons who will be in this age group in 1985 were not yet born in 1968.

That age group expanded very greatly during the past several years—from 24.5 million in 1955 to 35.9 million in 1965, a 46 percent increase in one decade. During the 1965-75 period this age group will increase by another 16 percent—

and then level off with no significant change during the next decade. In other words the period of the rapid expansion of the number of persons in this age group is nearing the end—until after 1985 when there probably will be another sharp rise.

The actual number of persons in this age range will increase from 35.9 million to 39.8 million in 1970 and then reach a peak of nearly 42 million in 1975. This will be followed by a leveling off at 40 to 42 million and then probably will be followed by a sharp increase up to a new plateau of perhaps 50 million in the year 2000.

6. *No significant increase in the number of children under age 10 until after 1975.* This is the most speculative of all projections on the age mix of the population since none of the children who will be in this age group in 1985 will be born until 1975 and later. For comparison purposes it should be noted that the number of children in the 0-9 age group hovered around 20 million between 1910 and 1940 (reaching a peak of 24 million in 1930), rose to 29 million in 1950, and then shot up to 39 million in 1960. A slower rate of increase brought this total to 41 million in 1965.

The Series C projections of the Census Bureau suggest this total will be only 40 million in 1975 and then rise sharply to 51 million in 1985. The more optimistic Series B projections put these totals at 44.5 million in 1975 and 58.4 million in 1985. An estimate of 40 million in 1975 followed by a sharp increase during the next decade now appears probable.

7. *The median age of the population will drop only slightly after 1970.* The median age of the population (median means one half above and one half below) dropped from 30.2 years in 1955 to 27.9 in 1965 and is expected to be down to 27.2 years in 1970. Thereafter it probably will drop very slowly if at all.

8. A continued increase in the number of widows. This is now becoming a factor that deserves special consideration. Heretofore this was a subject that was most visible in the parishes located in the small towns. It was not unusual to find 30 to 40 percent of the adult membership of one of these congregations to be widowed. Many were women who had spent most of their lives on the farm and moved to town when their children took over operation of the family farm or when their husbands died.

The increase in the number of widows has been very rapid during the past 75 years. Between 1890 and 1965 the number of residents of the United States tripled (the actual increase was 208 percent). The number of widowed men increased by only 162 percent, while the number of widowed women nearly quadrupled with an *increase* of 298 percent. In one sense these figures overstate the situation somewhat, since the percentage of women age 14 and over who are widowed decreased from 15.9 percent in 1890 to 12.5 percent in 1965.

On the other hand, however, during the past quarter-century the *number* of widowed men held fairly constant at about 2.1 million, while the number of widowed women increased from 5.7 million to 8.8 million—an increase of 3.1 million. Nearly one million of these widows have children under age 18. About 3.3 million widowed women are under age 65, while approximately one-half of the women who have passed their sixty-fifth birthday are widowed. About one-fifth of all women are widows when they reach their sixtieth birthday.

One way to illustrate what has been happening is to note that in 1920 the life expectancy for women was exactly one year greater than for men. By 1966 this difference had increased to seven years. Between 1920 and 1966 the life expectancy of the average 40-year-old man was extended by one and one-half years—from 30 to 31.6 years. For the average 40-year-old woman it was lengthened by nearly seven years—from 31 to 37.6 years.

IMPLICATIONS

Possibly the most far-reaching implication of these changes in the age composition of the American population will be felt in the central cities of the nation's large metropolitan areas. The exodus of middle and upper income Caucasians from the central cities is a well-known trend.

Who replaces these people in the central city as they move out to the suburbs? Historically it has been the newcomers to the urban scene—the European immigrant, the Southern Negro, the person born and reared in rural America, and the Puerto Rican. For many northern cities, especially those east of the Mississippi River, these sources of migration are drying up. The Census Bureau estimates that the immigration from abroad will average 300,000 to 400,000 annually (an annual average equal to 0.3 percent of the urban population) compared to an average of over 900,000 per year during the first 14 years of this century (an annual average equal to 2.5 percent of the urban population). The immigration from abroad will not replenish the population of the central cities.

Well over one-half of the Negro population of the nation now live in the large central cities, and another one-fourth live in other urban areas. This source of newcomers to the central cities also is rapidly drying up. (In Cleveland, for example, the net Negro in-migration averaged 5,500 per year during the 1950's; during the first half of the 1960's this figured dropped to a minus 260!) Most of the rural whites who are going to move to the cities have already done so. (The farm population of the United States dropped from 30 million in 1941 to 24 million in 1949 to 19 million in 1955 to 11 million in 1968. It is hard to believe that it will drop below 6 to 8 million.) While the migration from Puerto Rico has fluctuated, there is little reason to expect this will be a major source of newcomers to the central city—there are only 2.5 million people living on the island. In other words it is unlikely that the traditional sources of migration will be adequate to replace those who move out of the central cities.

Who will be the new migrants to the central cities during the next two decades? The most highly visible possibility is that this replacement population will be drawn from the rapidly growing number of households headed by persons in the 20-34 age group. It appears very possible that many of these young people will choose to live in the central city during their early twenties and the first years of their married life. This possibility rests heavily upon the assumption that suitable housing will be available in the necessary quantities at the appropriate locations in the central cities and that the central city will be a safe and attractive place in which to reside.

In numerical terms this possibility appears to be more impressive than the often repeated expectation that persons in the age 50 and older group will come flocking back into the central city after their children have left the nest and the big yard that was an asset begins to be regarded as a liability. Between 1965 and 1985 the increase in the age 50 and over group will be 11 million persons. The increase in the number of persons age 20-34 will be 25 million.

The possibility that many of the older persons mentioned above will move back into the central city should not be discounted. *If* a substantial share of the replacement population for the central city comes largely from these two age groups, some interesting questions will be raised about the role of existing congregations in the central cities and also about the appropriate emphasis for new church development. One of the most interesting areas for speculation about the future role of existing congregations in the central city arises out of two facts. First, if there is a large scale movement of urbanites back into the central city, regardless of their age most of them will be Caucasians. Second, a rapidly increasing proportion of the congregations now meeting in the central city are composed of Negroes. Will the 1970's see a large-scale effort to racially integrate what are now Negro churches? Or will newly organized white congregations buy the property now owned by Negro congregations? Or will there be a new wave of church building in the central cities? Or will the new congregations function without the traditional building?

A second important aspect of this trend centers on the subject of leadership and clientele for the parish church. Many different studies have revealed that persons in the 35-65 age range, and especially those in the 35-55 age range, are the most active members of the typical parish. They are the most regular in their attendance at worship, they supply most of the institutional maintenance needs of the local church for volunteer leadership, they supply much of the money needed to operate the institution, and they constitute the clientele for many of the church's services and program.

During the next decade the number of Americans in the 35-55 age group will decrease slightly, and even the larger 35-65 age group will form a sharply diminishing proportion of the total population—from 35 percent in 1950 to 33 percent in 1965 to 30 percent in 1975 to 29 percent in 1985. The inevitable increase in the total number of churches will mean that a relatively constant number of persons in the 35 to 55 age group will be divided among an increasing number of congregations.

It has become a truism in Protestant circles that the churches have great difficulty in reaching persons in the 20-34 age range and especially those in the 20-29 age range. During the next two decades this will be the fastest growing age group in the total population. This suggests that the churches should be greatly concerned over the relative ineffectiveness of their efforts to relate to this segment of the American population. In terms of the age mix of the population, this 20-34 age group should be the top priority on the churches' agenda.

One important implication of this increase in the 20-34 age group will be felt first in the seminaries as enrollments climb, and later in the parish and the denominations. The 1970's will see the ordination of a large number of young men with new ideas, new points of view, and a new degree of openness to change. This will produce new tensions within ecclesiastical circles.

Perhaps the most important aspect of this trend is the probability that a very large percentage of this growing number of young persons will not be living in single family homes in suburban residential neighborhoods. (See Chapter 8 for further detail on this point.) The impact of this possibility may be reduced if there is a large wave of young seminary graduates coming into the parish ministry.

Another item of direct concern to both the local churches and the denominations concerns housing for the growing number of elderly persons. The rapid increase in the number of elderly persons already has produced a large number of specialized housing developments such as retirement villages and church-sponsored housing projects for the elderly. This raises a couple of very important questions for churchmen. First, should the churches encourage this geographical isolation of the elderly? Second, should the churches try to minister to the residents of homes for the elderly with a specialized ministry directed solely to the elderly? Or should the churches attempt to integrate these residents into congregations that cover a wider age span?

One of the most obvious implications of this trend concerns the church school and the matter of church school facilities. It appears that for at least five or six years any new demands for large-scale expansion of church school facilities probably will be caused by a geographical redistribution of the population rather than by any large increase in the total number of children enrolled. This contrasts with the church school building boom of 1950-65, which was in response to a major geographical redistribution of young families *and* a 50 percent increase in the number of persons in the 5-14 age group. There will be practically no change in the number of persons in this age group between 1968 and 1977.

The changing age mix of the population also is of great interest to those concerned with new church development. Five points merit special attention here.

1. Much of the demand for new church development that occurred between 1945 and 1965 was produced by an increase in the number of persons age 35-55 and by the geographical relocation of this age group. These pressures for new church development probably will be less strong during the next two decades, since there will be no increase in the size of this age group until after 1980.

2. The two new bulges in the age distribution of the population—over 65 and 20-34—plus the increase in the number of widows should encourage the denominations to consider either (a) placing a heavy emphasis on specialized ministries, on unconventional evangelism, and on new approaches to reaching people with the gospel, or (b) en-

couraging and assisting existing parishes to minister to a broader age range.

3. The number of households where the head of the household is in the 35-55 age range will remain almost constant during the next 15 years. The number of households where the head of the household is under 35 will increase by over 60 percent during the same period. It is reasonable to expect that many of these new and younger households will be found in apartment buildings. The question of how the churches reach people in apartments must be reopened. (See pages 116-21 for additional detail on this point.)

4. There may be a sharp increase in the demand for new church development geared to the young married couple (age 25-44) with children beginning around 1975 to 1980. The extent of this demand will be determined in large part by where these new families establish their households. If they begin married life in the central city they may be served by existing churches—perhaps by what are now predominantly Negro congregations, perhaps by newly organized congregations.

If they begin their married life in existing suburban housing they may be served by existing churches, and the new church development programs will be geared to the older couples moving out of these homes and into new homes. If these new families seek newly constructed homes this will mean that the new church development efforts will be aimed directly at them. All these patterns probably will develop. Which will be the dominant one will depend on whether the large increase in the number of these young married couples produces a direct or an indirect impact on housing construction.

5. The increasing numbers of older persons coupled with the anticipated change in the economic status of retired people may create some unexpected conditions. Today a large

percentage of employed people regard social security as only one of several plans they have to insure that they will have economic freedom in their retirement years. One of their grounds for economic security is reflected in the growing prevalence of home ownership (the percentage of housing units occupied by the owner increased by one-half between 1940 and 1960—the *number* of owner occupied units more than doubled). The growth of private pension plans and deferred profit-sharing programs is another element in this trend. The number of persons covered by private pension plans increased sixfold between 1940 and 1965. The dollar reserves of these private pension plans increased nearly 30 times in that period. The dollar value of life insurance in force has increased sevenfold since 1940 and doubled since 1956. As a result of these and similar programs the vast majority of employed Americans who today are under age 50 can expect to be in comfortable economic circumstances when they retire.

Where will these older people live when they retire? Will this economic freedom influence where they spend their retirement years? Will the development of retirement villages turn into a large-scale trend? Will these people prefer to live in the central cities? Or will they mix in with the general geographical distribution of the population as has generally been the pattern up to now? Will these people have a major *direct* impact on new church development planning? While it is too early to provide a categorical answer to these questions, the growing trend of the American population to compartmentalize along economic, racial, age, and social lines leads one to believe that perhaps 10 to 20 percent of all new church developments may be directed toward serving this segment of the American population.

Finally, it should be emphasized that the people in the churches must avoid the risk of becoming so concerned with numbers and statistical trends that they neglect the reconciling role of the church. Hopefully the statistics in this chapter will help leaders in the churches identify the needs of the people and enable them to plan more wisely to meet these needs. If this is done, it may reduce the adverse effects of the various forms of the generation gap.

SUGGESTIONS FOR FURTHER READING

Epstein, Lenore A. and Murray, Janet H. *The Aged Population of the United States.* Research Report No. 19. Social Security Administration. Washington: Government Printing Office, 1967.

"Projections of the Population of the United States by Age, Sex and Color to 1990, with Extensions of Population by Age and Sex to 2015," *Current Population Reports.* Series P-25, No. 381 (December 18, 1967).

Wattenberg, Ben J. and Scammon, Richard M. *This U. S. A.* Rev. ed. Garden City, N. Y.: Doubleday, 1967.

PART TWO

BASIC DEMOGRAPHIC AND HOUSING TRENDS

5. THE NEW POPULATION BOOM

BASIC TREND

The population of the United States will in-crease by 60 to 70 million persons between 1965 and 1985—a larger increase than occurred between 1945 and 1965.

The population growth of the United States during the 1965-85 period is expected to exceed by a substantial amount the actual numerical growth during the so-called "population boom" of 1945-65.

The most recent population projections of the Bureau of the Census (Series P-25, no. 388, March 14, 1968) offer the traditional four series based on differing sets of assumptions. Series A is based on assumptions that include a birth rate similar to that which prevailed during the 1950's and a comparatively low death rate. The Series B projections assume a birth rate in the future similar to that which prevailed in 1949, 1964, and 1965. By contrast, Series C and D projections are based on a series of more conservative assumptions that include a birth rate similar to that of the period before the post World War II baby boom.

PROJECTIONS OF TOTAL POPULATION: 1970 TO 2015
(In thousands. Figures include Armed Forces abroad)

Year (July 1)	Series A	Series B	Series C	Series D
1966*	196,842	196,842	196,842	196,842
1970	208,615	207,326	206,039	204,923
1975	227,929	223,785	219,366	215,367
1980	250,489	243,291	235,212	227,665
1985	274,748	264,607	252,871	241,731
1990	300,131	286,501	270,770	255,967
1995	328,536	309,830	288,763	269,485
2000	361,424	335,977	307,803	282,642
2005	398,407	365,254	328,679	296,420
2010	437,851	396,012	349,947	309,661
2015	482,074	430,197	373,502	324,487

* Current estimate.
SOURCE: Table A, "Projections of the Population of the United States, by Age, Sex and Color to 1990, with Extensions of Total Population to 2015," *Population Estimates,* Series P-25, no. 388 (March 14, 1968), Bureau of Census.

Influences on This Trend

The rate of population growth is affected by a variety of factors, but six stand out and merit closer examination here.

1. Number of women of child-bearing age. The birth rate in the United States has dropped from 24.6 births per 1,000 residents in 1955 to 23.7 in 1960 to 17.8 in 1967. This was an even lower figure than prevailed during the depression years when the crude birth rate dropped to 18.4 in 1933 and again in 1936. One of the most important reasons for this decrease

was the fact that the number of women in the population age group 20-34 (four out of five babies are born to mothers in this age range) held steady at about 17 to 18 million during these years, while during the same period the total population was increasing. Since the crude birth rate figures are based on the total population this produced a sharp decline in the crude birth rate.

In 1975 there will be approximately 25 million women in the American population in the 20-34 age group.

In 1985 there will be 30 million women in the American population in this age group.

The number of married couples in the United States is expected to rise from 42.3 million in 1965 to 51 million in 1975 to 60 million in 1985.

Influence of New Birth Control Methods

The number of births in the United States leveled off at about 2.8 million per year in 1910 and, while fluctuating mildly, held remarkably close to that figure for 35 years. A new plateau of about 4.2 million births annually was reached in the 1950's. After reaching a peak of 4.3 million births in 1957 the annual total declined to 3.4 million in 1968. There was an especially sharp decline beginning in 1962. In the peak year of 1957 there were 123 births for each 1,000 women age 15-44. In 1960 this figure had dropped to 119, and in 1967 it was down to 89. The record low was 76 in 1936.

Circumstantial evidence suggests the largest part of this decrease in the number of births can be attributed to the more widespread use of effective birth control methods, especially the pill and intra-uterine devices, and to the apparent desire of younger couples to have smaller families—although there is some question about the validity of this last assumption. A reasonable guess would be that the number of births in 1967 was perhaps 300,000 lower than it otherwise would have been, simply as a result of the greater use of just these two methods of birth control.

Current estimates indicate that 6 million of the 33 million women in the 18-45 age range are using the pill. The Food and Drug Administration has estimated that this number will rise to 11 million by 1985—and it probably will be closer to 20 million.

Despite the growing use of birth control pills and devices, the tremendous increase in the number of young married couples is expected to produce new records in the number of babies born each year. The medium high projection of the Census Bureau places the number of births at 5.4 million in 1975, while the medium low estimate is 4.7 million for 1975. Either one would be a record high. The lowest official estimate for 1975 is 4 million births—20 percent above the 1967 total.

Age at First Marriage

From 1890 to 1956 the age at which young people married dropped steadily—from a median of 22.0 years for women and 26.1 years for men in 1890 to 20.1 years and 22.5 years respectively in 1956. The averages then rose to 20.6 and 23.1 in 1967—the highest since 1948.

This has had the effect of slowing the rate of new family formations and probably has had and will continue to have a minor depressing effect on the birth rate. The increasing percentage of 18-year-olds who go to college, the increasing number of college graduates who go on to graduate school, the increasing availability of effective birth control methods, and the impact of the military draft may result in a continued rise in the age at first marriage.

Percentage of Women Who Marry

The spinster is gradually disappearing from the American scene. From 1940 to 1960 the percentage of women age 35-44 who were married rose from 81 to 87 percent. In 1968 93 percent of the men and 94 percent of the women in the 45-54 age bracket either were married or had been married. By the year 2,000 this percentage is expected to reach 96 or 97 percent for women. Despite the increase in the size of the population the number of single women age 14 and over actually dropped by 3 million between 1940 and 1955.

Family Size

In recent years the general trend has been toward an increase in family size. Obviously if the tendency is for families to have more children, this will have an important effect on population growth trends. In 1968 American families averaged 2.7 children. Couples born in the 1906-1915 period averaged 2.4 children, while those born in the 1930's averaged 3.3 children. Married women born in the 1930's and the early 1940's have consistently said they would like to have three children.

In 1950 48.3 percent of the families had no children under age 18. This figure showed a consistent decline until 1963 when it bottomed out at 42.8 percent. It has since gone up to 44.3 in 1966.

The percentage of families with only one child under age 18 dropped consistently during the 1950's from 21.1 percent in 1950 to 17.2 percent in 1966. The number with two children rose from 16.5 percent in 1950 to 18.5 percent in 1956 and then dropped to 16.8 in 1966.

The number with four or more children nearly doubled between 1950 and 1967, rising from 6.3 percent in 1950 to 11.5 percent in early 1967.

Another important dimension of this subject is the almost total disappearance of the childless couple. In 1940 23 percent of the married women in the 30-34 age bracket were childless. By 1960 this proportion had dropped to 10 percent, and in 1968 it was down to nearly 6 percent.

There is some evidence to support the contention that the trend toward larger families has leveled off, and this appears to be most evident among younger couples. In 1959 one out of every four wives age 20-24 gave birth to a baby. In 1968 fewer than one out of five women in this age group had a baby. It should be remembered, however, that these young couples still have ten to fifteen years to change their minds about the ideal family size.

The net reproduction rate reached a peak of 1,765 in 1957 and then dropped slowly to 1,507 in 1964, a figure still well above the 1950 level of 1,435. It then plummeted to 1,288 in 1966, the lowest figure since 1946. (A reproduction rate of 1000 would mean that each generation is replacing itself— a rate above that represents growth. From 1930 to 1940 this figure averaged about 980.)

The number of children ever born per 1,000 married women age 15-44 dropped from 2,866 in 1910 to 1,904 in 1940 to 1,859 in 1950 and then rose to 2,520 in 1964. It then dropped off to 2,476 in 1965. Perhaps even more significant is the fact that the number of children ever born to women in the 20-34 age group was higher in 1964 than in any previous year since the Census Bureau began gathering statistics on this item back in 1910.

A minor but interesting reason for this is that women marry earlier and have children sooner than was formerly the case. In the early 1930's the typical bride had her first baby about the time of her twenty-third birthday, some 20 months after her wedding day. Twenty-five years later the typical bride was a year younger at her wedding, and the first baby came after 16 months of married life. In other words, she began the actual child-bearing cycle when she was about 16 months younger than was the pattern of her mother's generation.

On the other hand a recent survey by the Census Bureau of teen-age girls indicated that they expressed a desire for fewer children than was expressed a decade ago by women at a similar age who are now in the child-bearing age. The early evidence suggests that the brides of 1964, 1965, 1966, 1967, and 1968 are implementing this desire.

Death Rate

One of the two most important factors influencing the rate of population in the United States is the death rate. (Immigration, which once was the second most important factor, is now a minor consideration, since net growth due to immigration is expected to average only 300,000 to 400,000 per year during the next decade. During the first half of the 1960's net civilian immigration averaged 364,000 per year—twice the average of the 1940-49 era.)

While the death rate has dropped drastically in this century from 17.2 deaths per 1,000 persons in 1910 to 9.3 in 1955, it now apparently has leveled off at about 9.5 deaths per 1,000 residents per year. All population projections assume that the death rate will range between 8.9 and 9.8 during the next two decades. Thus it is not expected that a change in the death rate will have any major impact on population growth projections. (It is worth noting, however, that in several countries such as the Netherlands, Denmark, Norway, and Sweden the death rate is between 8.0 and 8.6. If the American death rate dropped to this level it would result in a significant increase in the rate of population growth.)

IMPLICATIONS

First of all, it appears that the Series B (medium high) or Series C (medium low) projections of the Census Bureau are the most realistic, and early indications suggest that the more conservative Series C table may turn out to be the closest to reality. Using these projections as a guide raises four points of general interest.

1. This means that the annual rate of growth probably will be well below the 1.6 percent to 1.8 percent rate that prevailed during the 1950's. During the first half of the 1960's the average rate of population growth was 1.4 percent per year, and in 1967 it was down to 1.1 percent.

It should be remembered, however, that insofar as the outreach of the churches is concerned it is not the *rate* of growth, but rather the actual numerical growth that is decisive. Using the rather conservative Series C projections means an absolute increase in the population of 58 million during the 1965-85 period. This compares with an actual growth of 54 million between 1945 and 1965. In other words the church building boom of the 1945-65 period was stimulated by an increase of 54 million in the nation's population, while the next two decades probably will see a popolation increase of *at least 58 million* persons. The Series B projections suggest a population growth of 70 million during this 20-year period.

One of the most important yardsticks in measuring population growth is the increase in the number of households. During the 1920-40 period the number of households increased by an average of 0.5 million annually, this rate climbed to an average of 0.8 million annually during the 1940's, jumped to slightly over 1 million during the 1950's and slipped back to an annual average of slightly under 1 million during the 1960's. During the 1970's the *increase* in

NEW CONGREGATIONS ORGANIZED

	1959	1960	1961	1962	1963	1964	1965	1966	1967
So. Bapt. Convention	—	487	526	399	422	429	343	188	N.A.
Reformed Ch. in Am.	11	10	11	10	5	5	5	9	9
Christian	n.a.	32	17	24	18	37	23	15	16
Am. Bapt. Conv.	44	32	28	27	30	20	19	16	N.A.
United Pres., U.S.A.	67	77	55	71	49	46	43	33	27
Ch. of the Brethren	11	11	5	6	8	4	5	3	4
Evangel. Covenant	6	1	14	9	7	8	5	3	N.A.
Methodist	151	170	176	171	137	126	100	77	72
United C. of Christ	45?	45?	29	29	29	23	22	16	16
Luth. Ch., Mo. Synod	100	104	104	92	92	94	94	70	47
Luth. Ch. of Amer.	74	87	79	70	74(61)	54(84)	64(82)	56(46)	25(51)
Amer. Luth. Church	37	80	51(54)	50(66)	53(61)	45(48)	66(66)	36(42)	26(38)
Presby. Ch., U.S.	39	39	35	34	31	31	31	24	28
C. of God of Anderson	70	60	63	62	55	52	50	55	52

Figures for the United Church of Christ represent *only* those new congregations started with the assistance of the Board for Homeland Ministries—as many more were started by conferences, associations, or "mother churches." During the three-year period 1958-61 the two denominations that merged to form the UCC started an average of 45 new congregations per year.

Figures in parentheses for the Lutheran Church in America and for the American Lutheran Church refer to new fields entered; other figures refer to formal organization of new congregations.

the number of households is expected to average 1.3 million annually. This is triple the average increase of the 1930's and 50 percent above the average for the early 1960's.

2. In recent years one new religious congregation has been organized in the United States for every increase of 800 to 1,000 in the population. (This compares with the existence of one religious congregation for every 450 residents of the nation.) If this pattern continues it means that over 60,000 new congregations will be organized during the 1965-85 period.

How many of these new congregations will be related to the mainstream of cooperative Protestantism? Recent trends indicate that the mainline denominations are organizing a decreasing number of new congregations per year.

At this point it would appear that the dozen largest cooperative Protestant denominations will account for no more than 20 percent of the new religious congregations to be organized during the 1965-85 period. In other words, those denominations which together include 50 percent of all Protestant church members and 25 percent of all Protestant congregations will start about 20 percent of all new Protestant missions. The significance of the difference between these two percentages may be greater than first appears when it is realized that today new churches are the most effective means of reaching unchurched and inactive members.

3. Since most of this increase in the nation's population will occur in and near the larger urban centers where many congregations already exist, it may be that the most important implications of this projected growth are (a) there will continue to be an increase in the average number of members per mainline Protestant congregation, (b) existing congregations will have to be encouraged to be more effective in reaching the unchurched and inactive people in the

community, and (c) small, long established congregations out on the rural fringe will be faced with unprecedented opportunities for growth and service. To many of the members of these small congregations the changes and new opportunities may appear to be very threatening.

4. Certainly one of the most important questions about this new population boom is, who will baptize these babies? The reason for the question is that the number of infant and child baptisms in the mainline Protestant denominations has dropped off at a far faster pace than the decline in the actual number of births.

Using 1957, the year of the record number of births, as the base year, there followed a 13 percent decline in the actual number of babies born during the subsequent decade. In the United Presbyterian Church in the U.S.A., however, the decline in infant baptisms was 38 percent. In The Methodist Church, the decline was 30 percent, in the Presbyterian Church, U.S. 30 percent, in the Evangelical United Brethren Church 24 percent, in the Lutheran Church of America 27 percent, in the American Lutheran Church 23 percent. Only in the Lutheran Church, Missouri Synod, among the larger Protestant bodies practicing infant baptism, was the decline in infant baptisms no greater than the decline in births.

For the members of the local church there are four important implications that merit careful scrutiny.

1. The first involves the question of the optimum size of a congregation. Much of this population growth will occur in the expansion of existing villages and small cities that now are served by two, three, or perhaps even a dozen churches. Frequently members of these existing congregations view an increase in the population of the community as an opportunity for institutional growth, and they may oppose the launching of any new missions. "Wait until we reach the

optimum size before you start any more new churches here!" is the cry often heard.

What is the optimum size for a parish? There is substantial evidence to support the contention that the *minimum* size for a congregation served by a full-time pastor is an average attendance of 100 to 150 at Sunday worship. An average attendance of less than 100 at worship usually means an inefficient use of ministerial manpower and frequently means that an excessive proportion of the total available resources are used simply to keep the institutional machinery running. Only a limited amount of manpower, energy, money, and time is left for mission, witness, and outreach. There also is persuasive evidence available to support the belief that when the average attendance at worship reaches the 250 to 350 range a second full-time professional person should be added to the staff.

Many observers contend that the optimum size of a parish is in the range of 500 to 900 members (or an average attendance at worship of 200 to 300). When this point is reached, is this the logical time to begin a new mission?

2. The second implication for the parish church grows out of the sharp increase in marriages. Too often a couple is married in church—and seldom seen thereafter by the pastor. From 1950 to 1965 the number of marriages occurring each year was in the 1.5 to 1.7 million range. By 1970 this annual total will pass the 2 million mark, continue to climb during the 1970's and then level off at a plateau of about 2.5 million marriages annually during the 1980's. This represents a 50 percent increase in the number of weddings celebrated each year during this 20-year period.

Will this be matched by a similar increase in the ability of the parish to relate to young married couples?

3. The third factor that should be studied by members of the local church as they consider the implications of this

new population boom is the regional distribution of the population. For many parishes this is far more important than national trends. The demographers in the Bureau of the Census predict that the greatest population growth will occur in the West and the South. The nation as a whole is expected to experience a population increase of 36 percent between 1965 and 1985. In the Northeast and the North Central states the increase is expected to be only 28 percent, while in the South it will be 37 percent, and in the West it is expected there will be a 60-percent increase in the population during this 20-year period.

Specifically, the Bureau of the Census expects that the state with the most rapid rate of population growth will be Florida (81.5 percent), followed by Arizona (80.6 percent), California (72.3 percent), Nevada (68.9 percent), New Mexico (57.1 percent), Delaware (52.4 percent), Maryland (51.7 percent), and Utah (50.2 percent). These eight are the only states expected to have a population increase in excess of 50 percent during this 20-year period.

At the other end of the growth spectrum West Virginia is the only state expected to experience an actual decrease in the number of residents, and it is predicted that in 1985 this will be only a 0.3 percent decrease from the 1965 total.

Ten states are expected to have a population growth of less than 20 percent between 1965 and 1985. These are Oklahoma (19.8 percent), Rhode Island (18.2 percent), Maine (16.5 percent), Kansas (17.4 percent), Kentucky (17.3 percent), Pennsylvania (15.3 percent), Nebraska (15.0 percent), North Dakota (12.8 percent), South Dakota (11.7 percent), and Iowa (11.6 percent).

The other 31 states and the District of Columbia are expected to experience a population increase of between 20 and 50 percent for this period. Seven of this group (Alaska, New Jersey, the District of Columbia, Connecticut, Colorado,

Louisiana, and New Hampshire) are expected to be in the 40 to 50 percent range.

4. Finally, churchmen through the nation should remember that more does not necessarily mean simply more of the same. A striking example of this fact can be seen in the pattern of immigration resulting from the new quotas. Quantitatively the number of immigrants from the Eastern Hemisphere is expected to rise from 103,000 in 1965 to 170,000 in 1969. Qualitatively the changes will be even more striking. In 1965 the nations in the Eastern Hemisphere supplying the largest number of immigrants to the United States were Britain, Germany, Poland, Italy, Ireland, the Netherlands, and France—in that order. In 1969 it is expected that Italy, Greece, Portugal, China, the Philippines, India, and Poland will head the list.

As the nation passes through this next generation of population growth, there will be qualitative as well as quantitative changes in the population. Some of these qualitative changes and their implications for the churches are discussed in subsequent chapters.

SUGGESTIONS FOR FURTHER READING

Brooks, John. *The Great Leap.* New York: Harper, 1966.

Bureau of the Census. "Americans at Mid-Decade," *Current Population Reports,* P-23, No. 16 (January, 1966).

————. "Summary of Population Projections," *Current Population Reports,* Series P-25, No. 388 (March 14, 1966).

Charlesworth, James C. (ed.). "The Changing American People: Are We Deteriorating or Improving?" *The Annals of the American Academy of Political and Social Science* (July, 1968).

Hauser, Philip M. *Population Perspectives.* New Brunswick, N.J.: Rutgers University Press, 1960.

Mayer, Lawrence A. "Why the U. S. Population Isn't Exploding," *Fortune* (April, 1967).

Simpson, Hoke S. (ed.). *The Changing American Population.* New York: Institute of Life Insurance, 1962.

200 Million Americans. United States Department of Commerce (November, 1967). (This lavishly issued report was published to mark the occasion when the population of the nation passed the 200,000,000. It is available from the Superintendent of Documents for $1.00.)

Young, Louise B. (ed.). *Population in Perspective.* New York: Oxford University Press, 1968.

6. THE GROWING NEGRO POPULATION

BASIC TREND

Between 1950 and 1985 the Negro population will more than double with the greatest increases being in (a) the under age 35 group, and (b) in several Northern and Western states.

The Negro population rose from 8.8 million in 1930 (11.6 percent of the total population) to 12.9 million in 1940 (9.8 percent of the total population) to 15 million in 1950 (10.0 percent of the total population) to 18.9 million in 1960 (10.6 percent of the total population) to 22.1 million in 1968 (11.2 percent of the total population). By 1985 the Negro population probably will be between 32 and 35 million, and Negroes will account for about 13 to 14 percent of the total population. In 1950 one American in ten was a

Negro. Today one American in nine is a Negro. In 1985 one in seven will be a Negro. (The definition of a Negro here is the commonly accepted one that a Negro is a person who identifies himself as a Negro.)

More significant is the comparative age mix of Negroes and Caucasians in the United States. While 10 percent of the whites are over 65 years of age, only 6 percent of the Negroes are that old. While 28 percent of the whites are under 14 years of age, 37 percent of the black population is in that age group. The number of Negroes under age 20 rose from 6 million in 1950 to 10 million in 1965. The median age of the Negro population dropped from 26.2 years in 1950 to 23.5 years in 1960 to 21.1 years in 1968.

While Negroes will account for only about 11 or 12 percent of the total population during the next several years, they now account for 14 percent of the persons in the 0-19 age group.

Up until World War II Negroes tended to live in rural areas. This has changed very rapidly. In 1950 63 percent of all Negroes were living in urban communities. This figure rose to 74 percent in 1960 (compared to 69 percent for the white population), and in that year only 7.9 percent of all Negroes lived on farms. In 1967, 68 percent of the Negro population, but only 64 percent of the white population, was concentrated in 220 metropolitan areas.

It is very difficult to predict the rate of growth in the Negro population because of (a) the relatively large proportion of young people in the Negro population; (b) the possibility of a change in the percentage of persons with one or more recent Negro ancestors who identify themselves as Negroes; (c) the inadequacy of past statistics—in 1960, for example, the official census enumerated about 98 percent of the resident white population but only 90.5 percent of the resident nonwhite population; and (d) the sharply declining

Negro birth rate. The nonwhite birth rate in the United States dropped from 34.1 per 1,000 population in 1959 to 26.5 in 1966. It appears that the decline in the birth rate among urban Negroes is even greater. In Cleveland, for example, the Negro birth rate dropped from 35 in 1954 to 21 in 1967, and the Negro birth rate in Cleveland is now only slightly higher than the white birth rate—despite the fact that in 1965 the median age for Cleveland Negroes was 22.4 years compared to 32.2 for Cleveland whites.

Despite the difficulty encountered in making projections about the rate of growth in the Negro population, it is possible to describe three important elements in this growth.

First, the Negro population of the United States is growing more rapidly than the white population. Between 1950 and 1967 the white population increased by 27 percent, the Negro population by 44 percent. While this difference in the rate of growth will decrease slightly during the next decade or two, the Negro population will continue to increase at a more rapid pace than the white population.

This is largely because of two factors. First, the death rate, which has been higher for Negroes than for whites, will drop more sharply for Negroes than for Caucasians. In 1900 the death rate for Negroes was 50 percent higher than for whites —25 deaths per 1000 for Negroes compared to 17 deaths per 1000 for whites. By 1965 the rates had dropped to 9.6 for Negroes and 9.4 for whites. It should be noted, however, that in 1965 the average 25-year-old nonwhite could expect to live for another 43.3 years compared to 48.6 years for the average white person. More important, in 1965 the infant mortality rate was 25.4 per 1000 births for nonwhites compared to 16.1 per 1000 births for whites. In addition, the chances of a nonwhite mother dying while giving birth were four times as great as for the white mother.

As black people receive better health care their death rates will decline more sharply than will the death rates for whites. The life expectancy for Negroes will lengthen more rapidly than for whites.

The other factor in the anticipated comparatively rapid population increase for Negroes is the number of women of child-bearing age. Between 1966 and 1985 the number of white women of child-bearing age will increase by 40 percent; the number of Negro women in this age bracket will increase by 65 percent.

A second important element in the growth trend of the Negro population is the age distribution. The black population is unusually young. In 1968 the median age for the Negro population of the nation was 21.1 years compared to 29.0 years for the white population. While this gap of 7.9 years in the median age for the Negro population is expected to shrink, the median age for the Negro population is expected to be six or seven years lower than for the white population in 1985.

Another way to describe this age difference is to note that in 1966 Negroes accounted for 11.1 percent of the country's population, but constituted 13.9 percent of the population under 20 years of age. In 1985 Negroes are expected to make up 17 percent of the population under the age of 20. In 1985 it is expected that one-fourth of the Negro population in the United States will be under age 10 compared to less than 20 percent for the white population.

The third important factor in this trend is in the geographical distribution of the Negro population. The proportion of all Negroes living in the Southern states dropped from 77 percent in 1940 to 68 percent in 1950 to 60 percent in 1960 and to 53 percent in 1968. The proportion living in the Northeastern and North Central states rose from 22 percent in

1940 to 39 percent in 1968. Between 1940 and 1966 the *net white* migration from the South totalled 930,000 persons. The *net nonwhite* migration from the South totaled 3,704,000 individuals for the same period of time.

In 1940 the states with the largest number of Negro residents were Georgia, Mississippi, Alabama, and North Carolina. There were approximately 1 million Negroes living in each of these four states. Texas was in fifth place with 925,000 Negroes among its residents. A decade later the states with the largest number of Negro residents were still to be found in the South with but one exception. They were Georgia, North Carolina, Mississippi, Alabama, Texas, and New York in that order. Each included between 900,000 and 1,100,000 Negroes in its population total. By 1960 the distribution had changed significantly. The states with the largest number of Negro inhabitants were New York (1.4 million), Texas (1.2 million), North Carolina (1.1 million), Georgia (1.1 million), Illinois (1 million), Louisiana (1 million) and Alabama (1 million). No other state approached the 1 million mark in its count of black people.

The demographers in the Bureau of the Census predict that in 1985 there probably will be 16 or 17 states with a million or more Negro residents. New York and California are each expected to account for nearly 3 million Negroes, while Illinois, Texas, and Florida will each have nearly 2 million black residents. A dozen other states—Georgia, Louisiana, North Carolina, Ohio, Pennsylvania, Alabama, Mississippi, Virginia, Michigan, New Jersey, South Carolina, and possibly Maryland—are each expected to have between 1 and 1.5 million Negro residents.

In both California and New York the Negro population *under 18 years of age* is expected to be well in excess of 1 million in 1985.

IMPLICATIONS

A look backward at the changes in race relations during the past 15 years suggests why it is impossible to predict the implications of the anticipated growth in the Negro population. It is possible, however, to lift up several points that should be of interest to most churchmen.

1. The increase in the size of the Negro population, the changing geographical distribution, and the movement to the suburbs of tens of thousands of Negro families means that an increasing number of previously all-white parishes will be confronted with the reality of racial integration.

While there was an increase in the racial segregation of housing in over one-half of the nation's larger cities between 1940 and 1960 and this pattern of increasing segregation continued in the first half of the 1960's, an increasingly large number of neighborhoods are becoming biracial communities. The combination of open housing legislation, the growth of the Negro middle class, and the change in the attitudes of many white persons suggests that the biracial neighborhood will be far more common in 1985 than it was in 1965.

This will present a major challenge to thousands of what are now neighborhood-oriented, all-white congregations.

2. Accompanying this increase in the Negro population is a strengthening of many organizations and institutions created and operated by black persons. The growing awareness by whites of these black-controlled organizations often has been accompanied by a rising respect for the vitality, the relevancy, and the importance of these organizations. The Negro church is the most common of these institutions organized and run by black persons.

Already this has presented many a white pastor with a difficult choice. When a Negro family moves into his community should he encourage that family to join his church? Or should he encourage that family to continue their membership with the church back in the community from which they moved? Where is the line between the desire for reconciliation and racial integration and proselytism?

This question will be raised frequently during the next 15 years, and it will be increasingly difficult to know that one has chosen the morally correct answer. Unless the racial integration of the churches becomes a two-way street with whites joining what were previously all-Negro churches, the black denominations and the black clergy will be severely threatened. This will leave many black leaders with no alternative but to oppose all Negro traffic on this one-way street.

3. One of the lessons that has come out of the past two decades of experience in new church development is that a new mission has more flexibility and is more open to innovation than an old established parish.

Among other things this means that one of the best ways to achieve racial integration in the local church is to organize new missions that are biracial from the beginning. The Southern Presbyterian Church and the United Church of Christ have been especially effective in this, and their experiences suggest that a major goal in new church development should be to maximize the number of biracial missions that are launched.

4. Until the mid-1960's Negro churches were greatly underrepresented in most city, metropolitan, and state councils of churches. Despite the recent efforts to alter this pattern, the white churches and white churchmen have continued to dominate these organizations.

A comparison of this pattern with the fact that in 1968 54 percent of the Negro population but only 27 percent of the white population lived in the central cities of the nation's metropolitan areas makes it apparent why white churchmen in the metropolitan centers must give more attention to this issue.

5. The increase in the Negro population, the rapidly growing number of young Negroes concerned with the issue of identity, and the worldwide rebirth of nationalism have accelerated a natural desire for the power of self-determination among Americans of African descent.

One of the great challenges to the churches of the nation, both white and black, is to recognize, understand, interpret, and support this growing demand for the power of self-determination among Negroes.

6. During the past 15 years the nature, composition, and goals of the civil rights movement have changed dramatically. One of the challenges to the churches has been to interpret this changing pattern to both the members and the larger community. The pattern will continue to change, and the churches will be challenged to keep abreast of these changes. This will become an even more complex and difficult task with the passage of time.

Perhaps the best example of this increasing complexity can be found in looking at the interrelated issues of race and poverty. Many churchmen had great difficulty in understanding and supporting the civil rights movement of the 1954-64 period because the politicization of this issue was so closely tied in to the highly emotional matter of racial prejudice. Now with the politicization of the problem of poverty and the emergence of a biracial coalition of welfare rights groups the churches must interpret an issue that is complicated by the presence of two emotionally explosive factors—prejudice against the Negro and prejudice toward the poor.

As the problem of justice for the poor, both black and white, supplants the civil rights movement as the gravest domestic issue, the churches of both races will find this to be a divisive issue.

7. Perhaps the most frustrating product of the growth of the Negro population will be the widening gap between the parish church and the Negro youth. This will be felt most severely by members of predominantly Negro congregations, but it is a subject that should be high on the list of concerns of all churchmen. In 1975 there will be 3 million Negro boys and men in the 15 to 25 age group. That is over twice as many as there were in this age group in 1955. If the growth in alienation, in dissatisfaction with the institutions and structures of society, in militancy, and in a desire for self-determination parallels this growth in numbers it will present a tremendous challenge to the churches as agents of reconciliation.

8. In 1968, 20 years after the United States Supreme Court ruled that real estate covenants that discriminated against Negroes were not legally enforceable, the American Negro still was burdened with tremendous handicaps. In 1948 the unemployment rate among Negro teen-agers was slightly lower than among white teen-agers. During the next two decades the unemployment rate for white youth doubled; for Negro youth it quadrupled. In 1953 the Negro unemployment rate was 71 percent higher than for whites; in 1968 it was 118 percent higher. Among whites the unemployment rate tends to decline as education increases, but for Negroes the unemployment rate for the high school graduate has been nearly as high as for the person with less than an eighth grade education.

In 1968 91 percent of the white families had a male head compared to 75 percent of the Negro families. In 1966 the Negro family with a male head averaged 1.98 children compared to 1.38 for the white family with a male head—but the smaller white family averaged $7,498 in income compared to only $4,593 for the larger Negro family. In the white family with children under 18 years of age the chances were over nine out of ten that both parents were present—in the Negro family the chances were seven out of ten.

In 1960, according to a study by Tempo, an urban white father of three had to earn at least $4,200 to afford standard housing. The higher price charged Negroes for decent housing meant that the nonwhite father of three had to earn at least $5,500 to be able to afford comparable quarters.

For the churches these and dozens of similar statistics mean that the struggle for racial and economic justice has not yet been won. As the Negro population increases, and as the number of young Negroes old enough to enter the labor market doubles in a single decade the struggle for equal opportunity in the marketplace will need all the support that the churches can mobilize.

SUGGESTIONS FOR FURTHER READING

Brink, William and Harris, Louis. *Black and White.* New York: Simon and Schuster, 1967.

Downs, Anthony. "Alternative Futures for the American Ghetto," *Daedalus* (Fall, 1968).

Greenwood, Elma. *How Churches Fight Poverty.* New York: Friendship Press, 1967.

Miller, Herman P. and Newman, Dorothy K. "Social and Economic Conditions of Negroes in the United States," *Current Population Reports.* Bureau of the Census, Series P-23 (October, 1967), p. 24.

Rainwater, Lee and Yancey, William L. *The Moynihan Report and the Politics of Controversy.* Cambridge: The M.I.T. Press, 1967.

Schaller, Lyle E. "Lessons In Integration," *Planning for*

Protestantism in Urban America. Nashville: Abingdon Press, 1965.

Taeuber, Karl F. and Taeuber, Alma F. *Negroes In Cities.* Chicago: Aldine Publishing Company, 1965.

"The American Negro," *Daedalus* (Fall, 1965 and Winter, 1966).

Wildavsky, Aaron. "The Empty-head Blues: Black Rebellion and White Reaction," *The Public Interest* (Spring, 1968).

Wilson, Robert L. and Davis, James H., Jr. *The Church in the Racially Changing Community.* Nashville: Abingdon Press, 1966.

32.414

7. AMERICANS ON THE MOVE

BASIC TREND

The rate of migration and mobility is not expected to change significantly during the next 20 years, but the cumulative effect of continued migration will cause important changes.

The rates of migration (moves across a county line) and of mobility (moves within the county) of the American people is a cause of considerable confusion among churchmen. One reason for this is the circulation of statistics that suggest that the American people are a highly mobile group and that mobility is increasing. Another is the failure to distinguish the differences in rates among various segments of the population. A third reason for the confusion is that it is easy to draw inaccurate conclusions from accurate data.

For example, it is accurate to state that nearly 20 percent of the people move each year. In the period from March, 1966 to March, 1967 18.3 percent of the residents of the

United States changed addresses. (Incidentally, this was the lowest percentage in two decades.) It is highly inaccurate, however, to jump to the conclusion that in five years everyone will move, or that in the average congregation one-fifth of the members will be moving away and taking their names off the membership roll.

A more accurate elaboration of the basic fact that nearly one-fifth of the population moves each year would be to add that (1) about one-third of the people account for most of the moves that occur in any single ten-year-period, and the other two-thirds of the population tend to move on the average of only once every eight or nine years; and (2) that when most people change addresses they do not move far enough away to make it necessary to transfer their church membership; usually they remain in the same parish.

Before going on to look at the implications of this trend it may be helpful first to review the facts, to describe the trend in greater detail, and to note any major changes in the patterns of migration and mobility.

During each of the past 20 years approximately 80 percent of the people did not move during that 12-month period; about 12 percent moved but stayed within the same county; another 6 percent moved across the county line but stayed within the same state; and slightly over 3 percent moved across a state line. Two-thirds of those crossing a state line moved to a noncontiguous state—they crossed at least two state lines.

The people who move each year are drawn from one-half of the population while the other one-half tends to be very stable. In the 1935-40 period three out of five Americans did not change their place of residence. In the longer 1940-47 period, when the war and its aftereffects caused an unusually large number of moves, two out of five Americans did not move.

Currently, according to the best available estimates, the cumulative effect of the fact that one-fifth of the people move each year is that over a five-year period this will mean that somewhat less than one-half of the people change address. A majority of those who move in any given year probably will move at least once during the next four years.

Another index suggests the American population is less mobile than many churchmen believe is the fact that about 14 percent of the people have been living in the same house for over 20 years, while another 13 percent have been in the same house for at least a decade.

There has been only a slight variation in the general trend. The two major variations are (1) in 1966-67 the percentage of people who moved dropped from the usual range of 19 to 21 percent and reached the lowest point in two decades, (2) this drop was due entirely to a decrease in the number of intra-county moves.

Another way to describe this trend is to note that in 1960 one-half of the people in the United States (age one and over) were living in the same house they had lived in back in 1955. One-third were in a different house, but in the same county, and about one-sixth had moved across a county line in that five-year period.

In each decade since 1870 the Bureau of the Census has found that about three-fourths of all native-born Americans live in the same state in which they were born. In 1870 this figure was 76.3 percent, in 1930 76.3 percent, and in 1950 73.5 percent, while by 1960 it had dropped only slightly to 72.8 percent.

Certain yardsticks suggest a decrease in the interstate mobility during the past century. One useful measurement is this question, "What percentage of the population moved from the state of their birth during any one decade?"

During the 1850-60 decade, the first for which comparable

data are available, the figure was 11 percent. Demographers estimate that this represented a decrease from the mobility rate of the previous half-century. During each decade from 1890 to 1930 this figure was approximately 7 percent, and then it dropped to 4 percent during the 1930's. During the 1940's this figure rose to 9 percent and stayed there during the 1950's. When one remembers that this figure includes military personnel and students leaving home to go to college, it suggests that the rate of interstate mobility for most older and younger Americans is really very low.

Today about 91 percent of the people have been living in the same state for at least five years—and approximately one-sixth of the other 9 percent are college and university students or military personnel. In Florida, the state with the highest in-migration, in 1960 three out of four residents had been living there for at least five years. In California it was six out of seven.

Only about one out of each six or seven persons who moves crosses a state boundary in the process, and only about 3 percent of the population move to a different state in a typical year. About 65 percent of all movers stay in the same county when they move.

About three out of five persons who do move in a given year make the move between June 1 and September 30.

What Are the Variables?

The most important variable in this trend is age. Those most likely to move are persons in the 20-24 age group (40 to 45 percent move in any given year) and those in the 25-34 and 1 to 4 age groups (28 percent move each year). Those least likely to move are persons over age 40 (10 percent move each year) and 14 to 17 years of age (14 percent move annually).

A second important variable is place of residence. Persons

living on a farm are only half as likely to move as persons living in a nonfarm residence. There is no significant difference between the moving rate of nonfarm persons living outside a metropolitan area and those living within a metropolitan area. Likewise people in the suburbs move almost as frequently as the people living in the central city.

In regional terms people in the West and South are more likely to be movers than those living in the North Central or Northeastern states. In 1966-67 only 13.5 percent of the residents of the Northeast moved compared to 23.7 percent of those living in the West, 20.7 percent of those in the South, and 16.6 percent of those in the North Central region.

Education does not stand out as an important variable, although there is a slight tendency for people with some college training to move more frequently than those with less formal education. College trained persons, however, are much more likely to cross a county or state boundary when they move than people in the same age group without any college training.

The greatest, and probably the most obvious variable is marital status. As one would expect, a very high proportion (85 percent) of all newlyweds moved within 12 months following the wedding ceremony. Over one-half (52 percent) moved during the second year of marriage, and two-fifths of those who were in the third, fourth, or fifth year of their marriage moved during 1967. Reflecting the age factor emphasized earlier, only one-tenth of those who had been married for a decade or more moved during 1967. Divorced and separated persons are twice as likely to move in any one year as the rest of the population.

To sum this up, the people who move least frequently are married persons past 35 years of age—the same group that is most commonly seen in church on Sunday morning.

A *Lifetime View*

Ten years after the fieldwork was carried out the Bureau of the Census published the tabulations of a special survey made in 1958 to obtain a profile of the lifetime migration patterns of the American people. The survey was limited to persons 18 years of age or older. It revealed a number of interesting facts about migration patterns. These can be presented most readily by a series of simple statements.

1. While less than one-eighth of the population in this age group was living on a farm in 1958, over one-fourth (26 percent) of the population age 18 and over had been born on a farm.

2. While 37 percent of the people in this age group were living in cities with a population of 50,000 or more, only 31 percent had been born in municipalities of this size.

3. One-fourth of the respondents, including one-fifth of those age 55 or over, had spent all their lives in the same community,* exclusive of interludes of less than one year in some other place of residence and exclusive of time spent in the armed forces. (Two-fifths of the respondents in the Northeast region had lived in only one community contrasted to one-fifth of the respondents living in the West.)

4. Only 45 percent of the respondents had lived in three or more communities for at least one year each (exclusive of time spent in the armed forces), and only 15 percent had lived in five or more communities for at least one year each. (In the West 29 percent of the people had lived in five or more communities compared to only 8 percent in the Northeast.)

5. Two out of five of all respondents were still living in the same county in which they had been born (including

---

* "Community" is defined as an area of residence, i.e., a political unit such as a city or county.

one-fourth of the people age 45 and over), and nearly three-fourths of this group had never moved.

MIGRATION PATTERNS FOR PERSONS
AGE 18 AND OVER
By Region of Birth

	U.S.	N. East	N. Central	South	West
No moves*	29%	40%	26%	25%	21%
Same County	10	12	13	7	12
Different County ...	28	23	29	32	33
Different State	11	10	10	12	11
Different Region	21	15	23	24	23

*Means no move out of the community in which the person had been born.

SOURCE: U. S. Bureau of the Census. *Lifetime Migration Histories of the American People* (Washington: Government Printing Office, 1968).

As can be seen by examining the above table, Southerners tended to move out of the county of their birth to a greater extent than any other group. In 1958 only 32 percent of the Southern-born persons were living in the county in which they had been born compared to 52 percent in the Northeast and 33 percent in the West.

Likewise Southerners were most likely to move out of the region of their birth while persons born in the Northeast were most likely to remain in the region where they had been born.

6. For the white population of the nation, age 18 and over, 7.7 percent had spent all their lives on a farm (for two-thirds of these this meant a farm in the same community), and 15.8 percent of the white population of the country had moved from a farm to a nonfarm residence (but less than one half

—44 percent—of these moved to a residence in a metropolitan area).

7. By contrast, 12.3 percent of the nonwhite population age 18 and over had spent their entire lives on a farm (for three-fourths of this group this meant a farm in the same community), and 21.8 percent of the nonwhites had moved from a farm to a nonfarm residence (but nearly two-thirds— 65 percent—of the non-whites moving from the farm did move to a metropolitan area).

8. The persons most likely to have lived in the same community since birth (except for service in the armed forces and for intervals of less than one year away from home) were: first, those *nonwhites* born in cities with a population of 500,000 or more (69.7 percent of this group had not moved from the city in which they had been born); second, whites born in cities with a population of 500,000 or more (44.2 percent had not moved out of the home community, and this figure was between 39 and 46 percent for each age group above 25 years of age); third, those persons, black or white, reared in a rural nonfarm home located *within* a metropolitan area (44 percent had not moved); fourth, individuals born in cities in the 50,000 to 500,000 population range (35.9 percent had yet to move out of the community of their birth); fifth, those born in communities in the 2,500 to 50,000 population range located within a metropolitan area (27.5 percent had not moved); and sixth, those born in a rural nonfarm home *outside* a metropolitan area.

Those *most likely* to have left their home community were those nonwhites born in communities in the 2,500 to 50,000 population range (80.5 percent had moved) and those born on a farm, either outside a metropolitan area (79.7 percent had moved since they were born) or on a farm inside a metropolitan area (77.6 percent had moved).

9. As a result of this migration of one generation of Ameri-

can people from one community to another by 1958 six important changes had occurred in the geographical distribution of the population age 18 and older.

(a) The number of people living on farms in 1958 was less than one-half the number of the nation's residents who had been born on farms.

(b) The number of people living in rural nonfarm residences within a metropolitan area (the Census Bureau's definition of a metropolitan area follows county lines and usually includes considerable rural territory) was two and one-half times the number of persons who had been born in such areas.

(c) The number of people living in the suburbs was twice the number who had been born in suburban communities.

(d) The number of people living in cities in the 50,000 to 500,000 population range was double the number who had been born in such communities.

(e) The number of persons, age 18 and over, living in the West in 1958 was nearly two and one-half times the number who had been born there.

(f) While 8.5 million nonwhites, age 18 and over, reported that they had been born in the South, only 5.8 million were still living there in 1958.

10. By contrast the number of persons in this age group in 1958 who were living in cities of 500,000 population, or in municipalities in the 2,500 to 50,000 range *outside* a metropolitan area, or in rural nonfarm homes *outside* a metropolitan area was about the same number as said they had been born in each of these three types of communities.

These figures suggest that while the *rates* of mobility and migration are not as great as is sometimes suggested, the cumulative impact can produce major changes in the distribution of the population.

While many of the implications of this basic trend may be obvious to the reader, it may help to lift up a half dozen for review.

IMPLICATIONS

1. The local movement of people (mobility), plus the Americanization of second and third generation persons, plus the tolls of death are combining to break up the old ethnic pockets that formerly were scattered across the nation in both urban and rural communities. This has reduced the need for the old ethnic churches, but it has created problems for denominational leaders who are responsible for helping the ethnic congregation change and adapt or dissolve. Since the death of the institutional forms comes long after the disappearance of the ethnic population pockets, this will continue to be an important responsibility for years to come.

2. While the regional migration is small in any one year (99 percent of the people who move stay within the same region when they move in any given year) the cumulative impact is great, as already 20 percent of the adult population lives in a region other than the one in which they were born. For some denominations this means a strong institutional pressure to move from being regional denominations to becoming national denominations.

The Roman Catholic Church, The United Methodist Church and, to a lesser extent, the Protestant Episcopal Church are the only denominations with a broad geographical distribution of churches across the nation. While some denominations, such as the three large Lutheran communions, the United Presbyterian Church in the U. S. A., or the United Church of Christ have a good distribution of congregations in most sections of the country, other denominations such as the Reformed Church in America, the Mennonite

Church, the Presbyterian Church, U.S., the Church of the Brethren and the Evangelical Covenant Church continue to be sectional churches.

This leaves these denominations with three alternatives. They may continue as sectional churches and watch their members either become inactive or join other denominations when they move to a community without a congregation of that denomination. Or they may attempt to become national churches through an aggressive program of new church development. This is the path being followed by the Southern Baptist Convention. Or they may enter into a merger that will make them a part of a national church. This is what the Evangelical United Brethren did. This is what is being contemplated by the Presbyterian Church, U.S. and the Reformed Church in America.

3. Apparently the varying mobility rates among different segments of the American population has had an indirect effect on new church development.

For easily understandable institutional reasons the tendency in new church development is to start new congregations in communities where the mobility rate is lower than average. The result has been that much of the new church development activity has been directed toward the less mobile segments of the population—Caucasians, the employed, persons over age 30, parents, homeowners, suburbanites, the self-employed.

This means that if new church development is to be used as a tool of evangelism more emphasis should be placed on new missions directed at the more mobile elements of the population. This will be both more difficult and more expensive.

4. The changing age mix of the population suggests that mobility rates may go up slightly during the next two decades. The two big increases in the population mix will be in

those two age groups (0-4 and 18-34) that are most mobile. Therefore it is reasonable to expect a rise in mobility rates.

Couple this trend with (1) the fact that the primary cause of moving given by 65 percent of all movers is their job and (2) the increasing employment and vocational mobility of the male population, and it is reasonable to expect a high "turnover rate" among young married couples in new missions during the next dozen years.

5. On the other hand, it is easy to overstate the mobility of church members. The change of address rate often is quite high, but the membership turnover usually is under 20 percent per year—in the average Protestant congregation about 7 or 8 percent of the persons on the membership roll will have joined during the past year, and some of these will be children of members. Congregations in metropolitan areas usually have a turnover rate in their membership rolls of about 8 or 9 percent per year—only a relatively few average more than 12 percent turnover.

Why is this rate below the 20 percent level for the general population? First of all, because it represents only membership turnover, not mobility—many members change their place of residence without changing their church affiliation. They move within the bounds of the parish. Second, the members of mainline Protestant churches tend to come from the less mobile segments of the population.

6. It should be remembered that migration is a two-way street. For every five people who move to Ohio from West Virginia there are two who move from Ohio to West Virginia. For every seven people who move from Nebraska to California, there are two who move from California to Nebraska. Among other things this means many parishes will be welcoming former members back into the membership.

7. Perhaps the most important implication of this trend for the parish is that it will mean a continued movement

toward developing a greater degree of heterogeneity in the congregation. As newcomers from outside the community; from other regions; from different religious, cultural, ethnic, and racial heritages come into the congregation this cannot help but reduce the homogeneity. As this occurs the differences among congregations in the same community or in the same denomination will continue to become less visible and less important.

SUGGESTIONS FOR FURTHER READING

Gaustad, Edwin Scott. *Historical Atlas of Religion in America.* New York: Harper, 1962.

U. S. Bureau of the Census. *Statistical Abstract of the United States, 1968.* Washington: U. S. Government Printing Office, 1968.

————. Current Population Reports, Series P-23, no. 25, *Lifetime Migration Histories of the American People.* Washington: U. S. Government Printing Office, 1968.

Wattenberg, Ben and Scammon, Richard M. *This U. S. A.* Rev. ed. Garden City, N.Y.: Doubleday, 1967.

8. THE NEW LOOK IN HOUSING

BASIC TREND

The next housing boom will be substantially different from the housing boom of the 1948-59 era.

Housing experts predict that total housing starts should average 2 million a year in the early 1970's—up from the 1.6 million average of the 1950's and the 1.3 million level of 1966, 1967, and 1968. During the 1960's housing was the only major industry that did not participate in the nation's greatest economic boom.

There are five major reasons behind this prediction for a sharp increase in the number of new housing starts.

1. There will be a tremendous increase in the number of new households formed as the people born back in the postwar years marry. During the 1970's the number of *new* households formed is expected to average 1.3 million annually—compared to an average of less than 900,000 yearly during the first half of the 1960's.

2. More and more families are owning and maintaining a second home. In 1965 approximately 3 million families owned a second home—and this excluded vacation homes used as income-producing property. The editors of *Fortune* magazine estimated that this number increased by 100,000 annually during the first half of the 1960's, by 150,000 a year during the second half of the decade, and will rise by an average annual figure of 200,000 during the 1970's.

3. The new drive to eliminate slums and to meet the goal described in the Housing Act of 1949, "a decent home and suitable living environment for every American family," will produce a far greater involvement in the housing market by the federal government. A major step in this direction was the housing legislation approved by Congress in 1968, with the goal of 26 million new housing units to be constructed by 1978.

This will have two effects on the housing boom. First, it will increase the rate at which substandard dwellings are scrapped. In the early 1960's an average of about 350,000 units were removed each year from the nation's housing inventory. In the 1970's it is expected this figure will average 500,000 units annually. Second, the increased activity by the federal government will be geared to help both middle and low income families. This is in sharp contrast to the 1950's when the major direct impact of the federal government's role was to increase the housing supply for middle and upper income families.

4. The rising level of personal income will stimulate the demand for housing. (See Chapter 10.) This will be felt in many ways. The rise in income has been a major factor in the decline in the average number of persons per household. The average number of persons per household dropped from 4.93 in 1890 to 3.38 in 1960 and is expected to be down to 3.2 by 1975. The three-generation household has almost dis-

appeared from the American scene. The number of one-person households rose from less than 5 million in 1950 to 10 million in 1968 and is expected to exceed 15 million by 1985.

The new age of affluence has also produced a phenomenon known as the "new house family." Just as there are individuals who insist on always driving a new car, there now has emerged a group of families who are not content unless they are living in a new house. Sociologists estimate there are now over 2 million families in this category.

The decentralization trend (see pages 23-30) is creating a demand for new housing out on and beyond the edge of the large urban centers. The most visible evidence of this is the "new towns" movement. Statistically far more significant is the demand for homes in the small towns and villages that are tied to the older urban centers by the freeway network.

What Will Be the Mix?

The housing boom of the 1960's will be different from that of the 1950's in that it will be larger—an average of 2 million new housing starts a year compared to slightly over 1.5 million annually back in the peak years of the 1950's.

A far greater difference, however, will be in the mixture of structures that constitute the additions to the nation's housing inventory. During the first half of the 1950's 86 percent of all new homes were in single family dwellings. By the mid-1960's this figure had dropped to 62 percent. Multi-family structures and mobile homes accounted for the balance.

Several experts have forecast that during the late 1960's and the early 1970's less than one-half, perhaps only 40 percent, of all new housing will be in the form of the conventional single family home permanently anchored to a specific location. A more conservative estimate is that for the decade from 1966 through 1975 about one-half of the new housing produced will be conventional single-family homes and the other one-half will be in rowhouses, two-family homes, apartments, and mobile homes. Contrary to the popular stereotype most of the multi-family housing has not and will not be in the highly visible high-rise apartment towers. In fact about three-fourths of all apartments have been in buildings of three stories or less—the two-story garden apartment complex is the most common type of apartment construction.

Another important element in the housing mix is the rapidly growing mobile home industry. In 1960, 103,700 mobile homes were sold (plus another 40,300 travel trailers). By 1967 sales had more than doubled to 241,000 units (plus another 122,700 travel trailers), and sales are expected to pass the 400,000 level before 1975.

Equally spectacular has been the change in the shape and size of the typical mobile home. As recently as 1962 the ten-foot-wide model was accounting for three quarters of all color. Six years late two out of three new mobile homes were at least 12x54 feet in size, and another 10 percent were double-width structures. By mid-1968 5.5 million Americans were living in 2 million mobile homes. While many mobile home owners are retired couples, four out of ten mobile homes are purchased by couples under the age of 35 years.

Most of these people are permanent residents of the community in which they reside—in 1968 over one-half of the mobile homes had yet to be moved from their first location. The average resident of a mobile home moves less frequently than does the typical apartment dweller. Neither the structure nor the resident is especially mobile.

As recently as 1964 it was news when mobile homes accounted for 16 percent of all new homes built. During the

1970's it is expected they will account for 20 to 25 percent of all new dwellings.

One reason for this change in the housing mix and the growing popularity of apartments and mobile homes is cost. By 1968 the new single family house selling for under $22,000 had become a very scarce item on the market. By contrast, the typical mobile home, completely furnished, sold for $6,000 with 20 percent down and monthly payments of $75 a month for seven years. The large, carpeted, extremely luxurious, expandable, air-conditioned mobile home could be purchased for $14,000 to $18,000. Likewise the cost of the average apartment built in 1968 was almost exactly one-half the cost of the average single family home constructed that year.

IMPLICATIONS

1. The most obvious implication concerns the increase in households, the rise in the number of new housing starts annually, the demand for new churches, and the question of who starts these new congregations. (See pages 69-71, 81-83, 237-38 for a more detailed discussion of this point.)

2. A more complex issue is the ability of the churches to reach and minister to the people who will live in the new housing. If one looks at this in terms of the housing mix, the issue divides into six questions.

(a) Probably a million or more units of new single family homes will be built each year during the next decade. Will the traditional methods of new church development be effective in reaching the residents of these homes? The experiences of many new missions started in single-family neighborhoods in the mid and late 1960's suggest the traditional methods are less effective than formerly. A very substantial proportion of these new missions are growing more slowly, leveling off in size sooner and with fewer members than was true of the missions started a decade earlier.

(b) How can the church reach the growing number of people living in the high-rise apartment buildings? Thus far no one has developed a good answer to this question.

(c) The most common type of multi-family housing is the garden apartment. Thus far relatively few parishes or denominational agencies have faced the unglamorous and very difficult question of how the churches can reach the residents of these units. Survey after survey has revealed that the residents of these developments are only about one-half as active in a parish church as the residents of single-family homes.

(d) The ramifications for the growing number of two-house families have been largely ignored. The typical two-house family may spend three months plus another dozen weekends each year at their second home. Frequently this is a cottage, a trailer, or a mobile home in a vacation area 50 to 500 miles from their first home.

What is the parish relationship of such a family? Who is their pastor? Which church will the children join? Which church will provide the opportunities for service and be the channel for new ventures in ministry and mission? The church "at home"? Or the church in the community where the second home is located? Or neither?

(e) A growing proportion of the new housing will be constructed for low and low-middle income families. There will continue to be a tendency to concentrate this housing in the central cities and the nearby older suburban communities. If one accepts the maxim that the most important single reason for starting new congregations is that a new mission has a superior capability for reaching people who are not active in any church, then it follows that someone should plan to launch new missions to reach the people living in this part of the mix of the new housing boom.

This raises immediately several questions. Who will launch these new missions? Who will finance these new missions? Will these new missions be expected to become financially self-supporting? Most important of all, is this the best way to reach the unchurched *and to carry out the reconciling ministry of the churches* in an already racially and economically compartmentalized society? Or would it be better to encourage existing congregations, including those located several miles away, to undertake this ministry of outreach and reconciliation?

(f) Thus far the typical local church has had very limited effectiveness in reaching the persons living in mobile homes. This cannot be tolerated. Is the answer to be found in specialized ministries to mobile home courts and parks? Or does this further stratify an already divided society? What is the core of the problem, and what is the answer? Does the answer lie in the hearts and the attitudes of the members of the local churches located near the courts and parks?

3. Another way of analyzing the consequences of this trend is to look not at the separate elements of the housing mix, but rather at the people.

A few years ago a study of multi-family housing in Dallas divided the residents into seven types: young swingers, young sophisticates, newly marrieds, families with children, the urban-oriented, the home-oriented, and the job-oriented. Many specialists in evangelism contend that any congregation seeking to reach the unchurched should concentrate, at least for a period of time, on a single target population. Does such a division as this one of the residents of apartments suggest a way of focusing attention on people rather than on buildings? It will require a greater input of energy and skill, but it may be a more effective means of executing the Great Commission.

4. One of the consequences of this new boom in housing relates to the mobility patterns described in the previous chapter and to the consequences of these patterns.

A University of Michigan study revealed that when a new home is constructed this has the multiplying effect of causing four households to move. In other words the construction of one new dwelling enables three additional families to move. This suggests that the anticipated sharp increase in housing construction will have a significant impact on mobility patterns and produce some increase in the mobility rate—thus reversing the decline registered during the tight housing market of 1966-1968.

Combine this with the decentralization trend described in Chapter 1 and the rise in personal income described in Chapter 10, and it suggests at least a slight increase in the turn-over rate in the membership of the local church in the 1970's.

5. Perhaps the most important issue for churchmen in this trend concerns the stance of the churches.

During the housing boom of the 1950's the churches concentrated most of their efforts and energies on responding to the decisions made by others. Perhaps the most urgent challenge in the new housing boom is to influence the shape and direction of this new housing boom. The last housing boom increased the economic and racial segregation in the nation. The new housing boom also will have a profound and lasting effect on American society. The churches would be well advised to consider these consequences as well as the impact on the institutional church. Perhaps as much effort should be directed to influencing the form and nature of this new housing boom as is allocated to reacting to it.

SUGGESTIONS FOR FURTHER READING

Abrams, Charles. *The City Is the Frontier*. New York: Harper, 1965.

Cohen, Morris. "The Coming Boom in Housing," *Fortune* (May 1967).

Goodman, Grace. "End of the 'Apartment House Ministry,' " *The Christian Century* (May 10, 1967).

Here Comes Tomorrow! By the Staff of the Wall Street Journal. Princeton: Dow Jones Books, 1967.

Schaller, Lyle E. "Who Is My Pastor?" *Church Management* (September, 1962).

"Segmented Demand: Is Today's Apartment Market Divided into These Seven Renter Types?" *House and Home* (April, 1965).

Smolensky, Eugene. "Public Housing or Income Supplements—The Economics of Housing for the Poor," *Journal of the American Institute of Planners* (March, 1968).

PART THREE

ECONOMIC AND SOCIAL CHANGES

9. THE GROWTH OF THE MIDDLE CLASS

BASIC TREND

The size of the middle class in the United States is growing at an unparalleled pace.

One of the most remarkable trends in the United States during the twentieth century is the continued increase in the size of the middle class. This change in the size of the middle class is also one of the most important factors underlying other changes in American society. For example, the recent rapid increase in the number of Negroes who can be described as "middle class" is one of the basic reasons for the divergence of opinion among Negroes on many contemporary social, economic, and political issues.

The changes in the size of the middle class serve as an index to the degree of social, economic, and cultural mobility in the society. These changes also underlie the changing level of expectations among the members of the different classes.

125

A college degree in 1969 has about the same social status implications as a high school diploma had in 1900. This affects the goals set by parents for their children.

Social scientists usually turn to either of two standards in measuring the size of a social class. One is to use percentages. For example, the top 5 percent of the population in terms of wealth or power might be described as "upper class" and the next 20 percent as "upper-middle class." The use of this standard means that the size of a class changes only with changes in the total population.

Another, and more common, method of defining the size of a social class is to use such statistical yardsticks as formal education, income, and occupational categories. While this method has some serious limitations, it does provide a means of measuring some of the most significant changes in society.

The Increase in Formal Education

According to the United States Office of Education in 1900 only 6 percent of the persons in the 20 to 24 age group had graduated from high school, and less than 2 percent had graduated from college. In 1967 over 75 percent of the persons in this age group had graduated from high school, 33 percent had gone on to college, and most of them will graduate. In 1975 this proportion going on to college is expected to reach 60 percent.

If the time span covered is reduced, more reliable comparisons can be made. In 1940, 27 million Americans (26 percent of the population age 14 and over) had gone beyond the eight grade. In 1967 this figure had jumped to 99 million (71 percent of the population age 14 and over).

In 1946, when the flood of returning war veterans hit the college campus, 22 percent of the persons in the 18 to 21 age group were in college. By 1965 this figure had doubled to 45 percent.

In 1947 only 4.7 million of the 94 million persons age 20 and over had completed four years of college. By 1967 this age group had increased by only 25 percent to 118 million, but the number of persons with four years of college had increased by 147 percent to 11.6 million. Even more dramatic is the increase in the number of high school graduates. This group increased in size from 33.5 million in 1947 (36 percent of those age 20 and over) to 64 million in 1967 (55 percent of those age 20 and over).

In 1940 1.5 million persons (equivalent to 15 percent of the persons age 18-21) were enrolled in the nation's colleges and universities. In 1968 this figure was 6.7 million (equivalent to 53 percent of the persons age 18-21).

What of the future? There is every reason to expect that the number and proportion of the American population having some college training will continue to climb. College enrollment is expected to rise from 3.6 million in 1960 to 7.4 million in 1970 and then go on up to 9.5 million in 1975 and 11.6 million in 1985.

The median number of years of school completed by the adult population (age 25 and over) is expected to climb from 10.7 years in 1958 to 12.1 years in 1970 and then move more slowly upward to 12.2 years in 1975 and 12.5 years in 1985. The proportion of adults with a high school diploma is expected to rise from 49 percent in 1965 to 68 percent in 1985.

In absolute terms the number of adults with four or more years of college will continue to increase from 7.0 million in 1957 to 11.5 million in 1970 to 15.5 million in 1975 and to 21 million in 1985. In percentage terms the proportion of adults with a college degree will double between 1957 and 1985. In 1985 16 percent of those age 25 and over will have had at least four years of college, and two out of every five of these will have completed a fifth year.

At the other end of the scale, while the number of persons age 25 will climb from 103 million in 1965 to 139 million in 1985, the number with an eighth grade education or less will drop from 34 million in 1965 (one-third of the adult population) to 20 million in 1985 (one-seventh of the adult population). In 1985 nearly three-fourths of those adults with only an eighth grade education will be past 55 years of age.

Occupational Patterns

Another index to social class and a measurement indicating the change in the size of middle class is occupation. Here the comparative statistics also indicate a continued rapid increase in the size of the middle class. Between 1920 and 1960 the proportion of the work force engaged in white-collar jobs rose from 25 percent to 43 percent, while the proportion of blue-collar workers dropped from 40 percent to 36 percent. The biggest change was the decrease in those engaged in farming—a decline from 27 percent to 8 percent.

Between 1960 and 1970 the number of professional, technical and managerial persons is expected to increase by 40 percent compared to an increase of 22 percent for skilled blue-collar workers and only 18 percent for semi-skilled blue-collar workers. No increase is anticipated in the number of unskilled workers—meaning a sharp decline in the proportion of the labor force in that category.

A longer term view reveals that white-collar, professional, managerial, and skilled workers rose from 16 million in 1920 to 41 million in 1965 and will reach 70 million before 1985.

Income Distribution

While a review of the trends in educational attainment and in changes in the relative size of occupational categories indicates a continued growth in the size of the middle class, the trends in income distribution are much less conclusive. While there has been a sharp rise in personal incomes (see Chapter 10 for details), there has *not* been any significant change in the basic distribution of personal income. In 1947 the richest 5 percent of the population received 17 percent of the nation's personal income, and the poorest 20 percent received 5 percent. Twenty years later this pattern had not changed significantly, except the share of the pie received by the poorest one-fifth of the population had increased slightly from 5.0 percent to 5.4 percent, and the second richest fifth had gained slightly at the expense of the richest one-fifth.

On the other hand, if one looks at absolute income, rather than the distribution of all income, the statistics do support the contention that there has been a rapid recent increase in the number of people who qualify as "middle class," and especially those who might be described as "upper-middle class."

Between 1950 and 1960 the number of persons with a taxable *annual* income of $25,000 or more rose from 300,000 to 567,000 and then shot up to 1,500,000 in 1968. The proportion of families in the over-$10,000 bracket rose from 2.7 percent in 1947 to over 31 percent 20 years later. After allowing for inflation by converting this to standard (1967) dollars the proportion of American families in the over $10,000 income bracket nearly quadrupled in two decades—from 8.1 percent in 1947 to over 31 percent in 1967. By 1985 this proportion in the over $10,000 income class will have passed the 50 percent mark, still using standard (1967) dollars!

The Growing Negro Middle Class

One of the most significant facets of this increase in the size of the middle class is the recent sharp rise in the number of Negroes who have moved into the middle class.

The number of Negroes holding white-collar jobs doubled between 1957 and 1967, and the pace of this trend is accelerating. The number of Negro lawyers in the United States increased by only 65 percent between 1900 and 1950; in the next decade the number increased by another 47 percent. The number of Negro physicians increased by only 18 percent in the 40 years *before* 1950; in the *ten* years following 1950 this number increased by 12 percent.

Between 1959 and 1966 the proportion of whites in the $7,000 to $15,000 income range rose by 50 percent; the proportion of nonwhites in this bracket doubled.

The proportion of nonwhite families who qualified as "middle class" rose from 7 percent in 1952 to 37 percent in 1968. (This growth in the size of the Negro middle class may be the chief threat to Black Power and may provide an important counterforce to the black separation movement.)

IMPLICATIONS

While it is impossible to predict all the consequences and implications of this trend, this growth of the middle class does suggest several points of significance for the parish.

1. While it is true, contrary to a popular stereotype, that the frequency of church attendance increases as the level of formal education or family income rises, it is probable that this growth of the middle class will increase the demand for a rational interpretation of the Christian faith. As the educational level rises the unquestioning acceptance of dogma will continue to be replaced by a demand for a more detailed explanation of the faith.

2. The supply of trained, well-educated, and highly skilled leaders in most communities will continue to increase at a

comparatively rapid pace. This will continue to reduce the authority of the pastor as a community leader. It will force the local church to be discriminating in its requests to people to accept positions of leadership. What once may have been regarded as a challenging position of leadership in the parish may now bore many of the members of this enlarged leadership group.

3. The local church, which once stood out as a training ground for persons learning to develop their natural talents as leaders and which still fulfills this role in some communities, must adapt to a new relationship to this larger and better trained community leadership group.

4. The rise in the educational level of the typical layman is creating a different relationship between the pastor and the layman. A generation or two ago it was widely assumed that the pastor was one of the two or three best educated men in the parish. Today it is not uncommon for a pastor to have many laymen in his congregation with a higher level of formal education than he has. Among other things this means the alert pastor tends to be more careful in expounding as an expert on a great variety of subjects.

It also means that the demand will increase for a pastor to hold both a college and seminary degree. (In the Protestant Episcopal Church, widely considered to have a well-educated clergy, one-third of the men do not hold both degrees. In some other denominations less than one-half of the clergymen hold both degrees.)

5. This increase in the level of formal education, the increase in income levels (Chapter 10), and the increase in discretionary time (Chapter 2) suggest that the future may bring a much larger role for the laymen in denominational and ecumenical policy-making bodies that heretofore have been dominated by the clergy.

6. The same combination of trends mentioned in the pre-

vious point also may lead to a sharp increase in the number of "tentmakers" who also serve as pastors of smaller or geographically isolated congregations.

7. In the past, social class has been a more important factor than race in the compartmentalization of the population. The recent rapid increase in the size of the Negro middle class thus creates new opportunities for the racial integration of congregations. Will this become a two-way street as middle-class whites join what were formerly all-Negro congregations? If not, if the racial integration of the parish continues to be a one-way street, what will be the impact on the Negro churches, the Negro denominations, and the Negro clergy? Will this increase the demand for "black power"?

8. One of the products of this trend that is already apparent is that the parish pastor is being confronted with a whole new set of counseling problems. A generation ago the struggle to make a living was the top priority in the lives of most people. The new combination of more discretionary time, higher incomes, and more education is causing more people to give the search for meaning the top priority in their lives.

9. The mainline Protestant churches have always had a strong middle-class orientation. Will this increase in the size of the middle class further accentuate this traditional bias?

Despite this rapid increase in the size of the middle class, in 1985 one-third of the adult population will not have a high school diploma, 20 million people will have had no high school training, there will be over 20 million blue-collar workers in the labor force. Will this trend harden existing class lines and make it even more difficult for the mainline Protestant churches to minister to these people?

SUGGESTIONS FOR FURTHER READING

Brooks, John. *The Great Leap*. New York: Harper, 1966.

Cordtz, Dan. "The Negro Middle Class Is Right in the Middle," *Fortune* (November 1966).

Demerath, N. J. *Social Class in American Protestantism*. Chicago: Rand McNally, 1965.

Jencks, Christopher and Riesman, David. "Class in America," *The Public Interest* (Winter 1968).

Komarovsky, Mirra. *Blue-Collar Marriage*. New York: Vintage Books, 1967.

Main, Jeremy. "Good Living Begins at $25,000 A Year," *Fortune* (May, 1968).

Uthe, Edward W. *Significant Issues for the 1970's*. Philadelphia: Fortress Press, 1968.

10. THE RAPID RISE
IN INCOME LEVELS

BASIC TREND

The level of income of American families is rising rapidly, but relatively few individuals or families have large quantities of accumulated wealth.

In terms of *constant* dollars (after discounting the effects of inflation) the median family income in the United States rose from $4,401 (in 1966 dollars) in 1947 to $4,479 in 1950 to $6,210 in 1959 to nearly $7,700 in 1967. From 1947 to 1957 the real income (in constant dollars) of the average American family rose by only $1,326. In the 1957 to 1967 period, however, the increase was nearly $2,000. From 1950 to 1967 the actual purchasing power of the average American family rose by 66 percent. By 1982 the median family income in the United States is expected to reach $15,000 (in 1967 dollars and projected on the 1960-67 rate of growth).

The percentage of American families in the $5,000 and over income range (again using constant dollars) rose from 41 percent in 1947 to 63 percent in 1960 to 75 percent in 1967.

In 1947 only 8 percent of United States families had an annual income in excess of $10,000 (in constant—1966—dollars); by 1950 this was still only 8 percent; in 1955 this figure had risen only to 12 percent. By 1960, however, this figure had reached nearly 19 percent and by 1967 had jumped to over 30 percent.

The dramatic recent rise in levels of income and in wealth in the United States can be illustrated by a variety of other statistics. For example, in the late 1960's the *average annual increase* in the gross national product exceeded the *total* gross national product of 35 years earlier.

In 1957 *Fortune* carried an article "The Fifty-Million-Dollar Man" and identified 155 Americans with total assets of $50,000,000. Eleven years later the same magazine ran an article, "America's Centimillionaires," and reported 153 Americans with resources worth at least $100,000,000. One-third of this group had not qualified for membership in the $50,000,000 club in 1957.

Private contributions to religious, charitable, and philanthropic organizations passed the $15,000,000,000 per year level in 1968 and are rising at the rate of nearly $1,000,000,-000 a year. Nearly one half ($7,000,000,000) of this total went to religious organizations in 1968—double the 1960 figure.

There is every indication that this rapid rise in income levels, which began in 1961, will continue in the future. A projection of the 1961-68 trend indicates that the number of families in the over-$10,000 annual income bracket will exceed the number in the under-$10,000 range in the foreseeable future.

ANNUAL FAMILY INCOME*

Year	Under $7,500	$7,500 to $10,000	Over $10,000
1959	38 million	8 million	10 million
1968	30 million	10 million	22 million
1975	26 million	12 million	34 million

* In terms of 1967 dollars, thus allowing for inflation.

In 1967 one-half of all American families had an income over $7,900. In 1975 this dividing line will be approaching the $9,500 level, and by 1985 it will be near the $18,000 mark —in 1967 dollars.

By contrast, a decreasing percentage of the accumulated national wealth—now estimated at $2,000 billion—is owned by individuals or families. The average total net worth of all American families in 1962 was only $22,588—despite the rising income levels. A rapidly growing proportion is controlled by pension funds, foundations, public bodies, corporations, and secular non-profit organizations. Foundations, for example, now have assets of $21,000,000,000 compared to one-tenth that figure in 1939. About one-fourth of all foundation grants are allocated to health, welfare, religion, and the humanities.

Pension funds have become a major consideration in the distribution of wealth. The assets of private corporate pension funds (excluding those managed by labor unions) rose from $15,000,000,000 in 1955 to $53,000,000,000 in 1965. Denominational pension funds now have assets of over $2,000,000,000.

Other financial institutions are also gaining control of a huge amount of wealth. The assets of banks jumped from $192,000,000,000 in 1950 to $437,000,000,000 in 1965. The assets of all savings and loan associations rose even more sharply—from less than $6,000,000,000 in 1940 to $17,000,000,-

000 in 1950 to $130,000,000,000 in 1965. A somewhat slower pace of growth was recorded by life insurance companies. Their assets doubled from $31,000,000,000 in 1940 to $64,000,-000,000 in 1950 and then nearly doubled again in the next decade, reaching $120,000,000,000 in 1960 and then climbing to $159,000,000,000 in 1965. The persons charged with the investment of these funds have become holders of great economic power in recent years.

Another way to measure the distribution of accumulated wealth is to look at savings. In 1965 personal savings by individuals totalled $25,000,000,000—compared to the savings of $84,000,000,000 held by business firms. In the space of a dozen years the savings of individuals had increased by 50 percent, while the savings of corporations had nearly tripled.

IMPLICATIONS

In looking at the general implications of this rise in family income and the distribution of wealth several factors stand out that merit consideration by anyone seeking to diagnose the implications of this trend for the churches.

1. Basically this trend reflects the expansion of general economic activity in the United States during the past decade. There are other important factors at work, however, in producing this trend. Perhaps the most important to the local church is the working wife. Back in 1952 in only 23 percent of the husband-wife households was the wife employed outside the home. By 1967 this figure had climbed to 35 percent, and in that year well over one half (59 percent) of all women in the labor force were married.

In 1966 the average family in which the wife was employed outside the home had an income of $9,200 compared to $7,100 for the family where the wife was not in the paid labor force.

2. This recent rapid rise in income levels is a new trend

without parallel in American history. Never before has the actual buying power of so many people risen so fast. This means the reaction time for the churches to respond to this has diminished.

During the economic boom of the 1920's, for example, the buying power of the typical American family rose by less than 20 percent, and for most families the increase was less than 10 percent. The average annual compensation for all full-time employees went from $1,424 in 1921 to $1,421 in 1925 to $1,489 in 1929—an increase of less than 5 percent in nine years. For manufacturing employees the change in average annual income was from $1,497 in 1920 to $1,508 in 1929. (It should be noted here that inflation was not a significant economic factor in the United States in that decade.) During the height of the boom from 1924 to 1929 the average weekly earnings of a coal miner rose only from $23.59 to $25.72, the average hourly earnings in all industries rose from $.66 in 1923 to $.71 in 1928, the average hourly wage in basic steel was $.41 in 1923—and it was still $.41 in 1929.

By contrast in recent years the average weekly earnings of the production worker in manufacturing rose from $75.70 in 1955 to $107.53 in 1965—an increase of 42 percent in one decade. (Approximately one-half of this increase was the result of inflation, and one-half represented an increase in real purchasing power.)

In the decade from 1947 to 1957 the median family income in the United States rose by 30 percent (in constant dollars). In the decade from 1957 to 1967 the increase was 36 percent (again in constant dollars). These figures contrast sharply with the 10 percent rise in the twelve-year period from 1929 to 1941.

3. Despite the widespread attention given to the problems of poverty in recent years, the number and the proportion of American families in the low income brackets has dropped

sharply during the past two decades and especially since 1963. Using constant (1967) dollars to offset the impact of inflation, the proportion of families with an income under $3,000 a year dropped from 28 percent in 1947 to 13 percent in 1967. There was a similar decrease in the proportion in the $3,000 to $5,000 bracket—this group declined from 30 percent of all families in 1947 to 13 percent in 1967.

The "poverty line," as defined by the Social Security Administration, varies with family size, the number of children in the family, the place of residence (farm or nonfarm), and changes in the cost of living. In 1967, for example, the poverty line was $3,335 for a nonfarm family of four and rose to $5,440 for a nonfarm family of seven or more persons.

In 1959 the number of persons below the poverty line was 38.9 million or 22.1 percent of the nation's residents. In 1967 this total had dropped to 25.9 million or 13.3 percent of the total population. The number of nonwhites living below the poverty line dropped from 10.7 million in 1959 to 8.3 million in 1967, although this figure had climbed to 11.2 million in 1963. In that year over one half of all nonwhites in the United States were living below the poverty line compared to only one-seventh of the whites. In 1968 one-tenth of the whites, but over one-third of the nonwhites were still below the poverty line.

4. On the other hand it must be added that while the number and percentage of low income families declined sharply during the past two decades, the poor are *not* getting a larger slice of the total personal income. If one thinks of the personal income received by families and individuals as a pie, what has happened is that the pie is much larger than it was 20 years ago, but the slices are still of about the same relative size. As the size of the pie increases, the visible difference in *actual* size—as contrasted to *proportional* size—also increases. In dollar terms the gap between the poorest

one-fifth of the population and the other four-fifths has widened even though the relative size of the slices has remained unchanged. This trend contains within itself the seeds of its own destruction.

Specifically, in 1935 the poorest one-fifth of the nation received 4.1 percent of the aggregate personal income. During World War II this rose to 5.0 percent. In 1950 it had dropped to 4.5 percent, and in 1958 it had risen to 5.1 percent. By 1961 it was down to 4.8 percent, and in 1966 it had risen only to 5.4 percent.

During the past 30 years the size of the slice received by the second poorest one-fifth of the population rose from 9.2 percent in 1935 to 11.8 percent in 1947 to 12.4 percent in 1966. The size of the slice of the middle fifth rose from 14.1 percent in 1935 to 17.0 percent in 1947 to 17.7 percent in 1955, and it has hovered around that figure ever since. The same trend applies to the one-fifth of the population in the next to the richest bracket. In 1935 this group received 20.9 percent of all personal income. By 1941 this figure had risen to 22.3 percent, and it has ranged between 22 and 24 percent ever since.

The greatest change has been in the slice of the pie received by the persons in the top one-fifth of the population. In 1929 they received 54.4 percent of the aggregate personal income. Ever since then the proportionate size of their slice of the income pie has been shrinking. It was down to 51.7 percent in 1935, dropped to 43.0 percent in 1947, and was calculated at 40.7 percent in 1966.

The biggest drop was in the relative size of the slice of those in the top five percent of the income bracket. Their share of the income pie dropped from 33.0 percent in 1933 to 24.0 percent in 1941 to 17.2 percent in 1947 to 14.8 percent in 1966.

It should be emphasized that this reduction in the size of

the slice received by the rich did not go to the poor, but rather was divided among those in the middle three-fifths of the population.

For the person seeking to understand the unrest that characterized the 1960's these figures offer important clues. For many people the most important aspect of this trend has not been the sharp rise in family income, nor the increased public attention focused on the problems caused by poverty, but rather the comparatively static nature of the curve showing the distribution of income. In 1947 40 percent of the families received 66 percent of the income pie. Twenty years later there had been only a very slight change in this pattern, as the top 40 percent received 64.5 percent of the pie.

While there has been practically no change in the lower end of the income distribution curve during the past 20 years —and only a modest change in the past 40 years—there has been a tremendous change in the awareness and the degree of concern over this continuing inequality. While the actual income of the poorest one-fifth of the population has increased significantly, they still divide among themselves only about 5 percent of this rapidly growing pie.

For the individual concerned with the poverty issue, race relations, and the plight of black persons the details of this trend explain why many Negroes contend that better employment opportunities, including an increase in Negro-owned and operated businesses, is an essential element in any effort to improve the lot of the black man.

5. In an era when race relations is one of the two most pressing domestic problems facing the nation, the differences in the income of whites and nonwhites must be recognized.

While it is true that in the decade from 1957 to 1967 the proportion of Negro families with an income over $8,000 tripled and the proportion of urban black families living in poverty areas dropped by a fourth, there is still a serious income disparity between blacks and whites.

In 1947 the income of the average (median) nonwhite family was 51 percent that of the average white family. By 1952 this figure had risen to 54 percent, suggesting progress was being made in reducing the disparity. During the next few years this figure dropped, reaching a low of 51 percent in 1958. It rose slightly, going up to 55 percent in 1960 and then hovered between 53 and 56 percent during the great civil rights struggle of the early 1960's. In 1967 it reached a new peak of 62 percent—but the gap is still disconcertingly large. For Negroes in 1967 this figure was 59 percent.

In 1967 28.5 percent of all Negro (and 27 of all nonwhite) families had an income under $3,000—compared to less than 11 percent for all white families. At the other end of the income scale in 1967 only 4.1 percent of all black families had an income of $15,000 or more—compared to 13 percent (up from 10 percent in 1966) of all white families.

Although nonwhites comprised only 12 percent of the nation's population in 1967, they constituted 32 percent of those classified as poor. Furthermore, from 1959 to 1967 the percentage of white persons living in poverty dropped from 18 to 10 percent—a decline of nearly one-half. By contrast the proportion of nonwhites living in poverty dropped from 55 percent in 1959 to 35 percent in 1967—a reduction of approximately one-third.

6. Since 1950 there has been a sharp increase in the number of families receiving income from several sources. As recently as 1951 over 71 percent of all families had income from earnings only. By 1966 this figure had dropped to 43 percent. Or to put it the other way around, the proportion of families with income from other than earnings—such as dividends, interest, pensions, capital gains—doubled from 29 percent in 1951 to 57 percent in 1966.

7. Unquestionably the most important implication of this trend is that the United States has moved from an industrial into a mass consumption stage of its life cycle. This has occurred at a point in history when most nations of the world are still in a pre-industrial stage of their history. For the person seeking to understand the role of the United States and of the American churches in the contemporary world this is of fundamental importance.

Other Implications for the Parish and the Individual

For the person in the local church there are additional implications that are varied and important.

1. This higher level of family income has opened up many new opportunities for most families in entertainment, recreation, education, travel, and other activities that compete and conflict with the traditional parish program.

2. Affluence enlarges the number of choices open to the individual, the family, the community, the congregation, and the nation. The churches have both the opportunity and the responsibility to speak to the ethical issues involved in making these choices.

3. This trend also suggests that in many local churches it should be possible to redirect some of the time and effort that formerly had been allocated to finances and institutional survival to new ventures in evangelism, mission, and witness.

4. These figures suggest that the finance and personnel committees in the local church should give serious consideration to the salaries paid the pastor and other staff members. In other fields of endeavor salaries have been increasing at the rate of 5 to 7 percent per year. What will the future bring? What has been the pattern in the local church?

If the salaries of clergymen rise as rapidly as those of persons with similar education, and *if* inflation averages only 1 percent per year, in those denominations with a minimum salary standard in 1985 the minimum salary for pastors will be at least $10,000 a year. *If* the inflationary pattern of 1966-69 persists, this figure will be closer to $15,000 or $18,000 in 1985.

The long-term trend has been for clergymen's salaries to rise at a much slower rate than the salaries and wages of persons in other professions and occupations. In 1939 clergymen ranked in that tenth of the population third from the highest in annual income. By 1959 they had dropped to the next to the lowest tenth of the labor force.

Basically, salaries for clergymen have risen at a slower rate than for people in all occupations or in other professions. The following table documents this point very clearly.

MEAN INCOME FOR MALES WORKING OVER FIFTY WEEKS

Profession	1939 Salary	1949 Salary	1959 Salary
Clergymen	$1551	$2607	$4159
Teachers	2399	3901	6157
Pharmacists	1886	4150	7096
Chemists	2785	5026	7978
Authors and Editors	3189	6113	8360
Social Workers	2143	3823	5850

SOURCE: Herman P. Miller, *Income Distribution in the United States* (Washington: Government Printing Office, 1966, p. 252.

Pastors, especially those in the upper income brackets, should be conscious of the inequities in the distribution of income received by clergymen. It was pointed out earlier that when the income pie is cut in the United States the poorest one-fifth of the population receive a slice equal to only 5 percent of the total pie, while the slice divided among the richest one-fifth is equal to about 41 percent of the pie.

How is the income received by clergymen distributed? In 1959, the last year for which data is available, among the clergy who were employed for at least 50 weeks that year, the one-fifth with the highest incomes divided up 36 percent of the pie, while only 5.4 percent was left to the bottom fifth.

By contrast, the teachers in the lowest one-fifth of the teachers' income range in 1959 received 8.2 percent of the total income received by teachers compared to 32.8 percent for the highest one-fifth. Among civil engineers the poorest one-fifth received 9.1 percent of the income pie compared to 32.8 percent for the highest paid one-fifth.

One of the less visible aspects of "income" that should merit the attention of every congregation with an employed staff is the matter of fringe benefits. There are two dimensions to this issue.

The first concerns the fringe benefits provided for lay employees. The vast majority of Protestant churches do not provide their lay employees with fringe benefits comparable to those received by persons holding similar positions in public or private employment.

While many do provide paid vacations for lay employees and some offer paid sick leave, relatively few have a pension program for lay employees, rarely does a local church provide health or life insurance for lay workers, and only a small percentage pay extra for overtime. Usually the churches with the poorest record on this issue are the smaller congregations, especially those that employ people on an hourly basis. The best record usually is found in the large urban congregations, which provide fringe benefits similar to those offered by large private employers.

This lack of fringe benefits for lay employees would not

be such a serious matter except (1) the wages and salaries paid by local churches frequently are below the local market level, and (2) many of the denominations to which these congregations belong have shown no hesitancy in attacking private employers for failing to compensate their employees adequately. This is one of several areas where the prophetic voice of the churches also should be addressed to their own shortcomings.

The other dimension of this issue relates to the compensation provided for the pastor. In recent years the compensation received by pastors has been increased in two respects. The more obvious is the increase in the cash salary—in many congregations this increase averaged 7 percent per year in the 1965-69 period.

In addition, or sometimes in lieu of an increase in the cash salary, many pastors also are receiving improvements in the fringe benefits accorded them. The paid sabbatical of three, six, nine, or twelve months for study or travel is becoming an increasingly common part of the total compensation, especially in those denominations in which pastors are called by the congregation. Even before 1968 when Social Security coverage became mandatory for nearly all clergymen, many churches were paying the entire cost of the denominational pension program as a means of encouraging the pastor to elect coverage under Social Security.

More and more congregations are adopting some systematic method for completely reimbursing the pastor for automobile expenses incurred while on church business. In addition an increasing number of congregations are paying part or all of the cost of a health insurance policy, reimbursing the pastor for expenses incurred in attending church meetings and professional conferences, providing a full month's vacation, and providing some form of allowance for books and subscriptions to religious magazines and professional journals.

5. The sharp increase in the number of working wives—and especially among those with small children at home—suggests that for many communities there may be a real need for the churches to offer a child care program five days a week and on a *fifty-two weeks a year* basis.

6. The relative decline in the number of families with accumulated wealth means that the single large benefactor no longer is a prime source for the congregation embarking on a capital funds drive. The trend described earlier is being reflected in the fact that the large cash gift is becoming less significant in these drives and most of the money is received from the families pledging a weekly gift.

7. Perhaps the point that deserves the greatest emphasis in the typical white, middle-class congregation is that this unparalleled rise in family income has been accompanied by an increasing geographical separation of the population along economic lines. (See Chapter 12.) The poor, both urban and rural, tend to be concentrated in poverty neighborhoods, and the middle and upper income families also tend to be concentrated in economically homogeneous communities. This geographical compartmentalization of the population on an economic basis, combined with the widespread tendency of local churches to draw their members from a relatively narrow social and economic strata of society, tends to make it very difficult for parishes to fulfill their responsibilities as agents of reconciliation.

8. Many of the tensions that are disrupting American society are a product of the widening disparity between the incomes of the poor and those of the remaining three-fourths of society. The median income of the family in the under $5,000 income bracket—and in 1967 28 percent of all families were in that income group—is less than one-third that of the

average American family. By 1975 it is expected to be only one-fourth that of the average income of all families. The income of the person at the eightieth percentile of the income range is still four times that of the person at the twentieth percentile. More and more low income people are becoming aware of these discrepancies and are refusing to quietly accept this inequity.

9. One of the most important implications of this trend for the churchman who is trying to reform American society, and especially for the black churchman, is that land no longer is the source of income, wealth, and power that it once was. The emphasis of some Black Nationalists on the acquisition of land, such as the setting aside of several Southern states for black persons, reflects an obsolete concept of wealth and income.

A much more realistic approach is the "Bread Basket" program of the late Dr. Martin Luther King, Jr., and the Rev. Jesse Jackson, which recognizes that the road to higher incomes, power, dignity, and wealth for black persons, is through knowledge, skill, and participation in the financial and distributive sections of the economy rather than the ownership of land.

10. This accumulation of much of the nation's wealth by foundations, corporations, and various other organizations, rather than by individuals, says something to the individual churchman who has the responsibility for raising money for a particular cause or task. Many of these custodians of wealth are recognizing the social responsibilities that accompany this role. Increasingly they are receptive to financial appeals from ecumenical or interdenominational agencies and from those developing a program directed at the social problems created by racism or by poverty.

This suggests that while the traditional parish and denominational programs must continue to be financed largely by the contributions of individuals, many ecumenical and inter-denominational agencies and certain new church-sponsored action programs can and should be financed from other sources. This would leave the financial resources of the parish and the denomination to be allocated to those activities which cannot be financed from other sources.

SUGGESTIONS FOR FURTHER READING

Bazelon, David T. *The Paper Economy.* New York: Random House, 1963.

Elman, Richard M. *The Poorhouse State.* New York: Pantheon, 1966.

Fuller, Reginald H. and Rice, Brian K. *Christianity and the Affluent Society.* Grand Rapids: Eerdmans, 1967.

Galbraith, John Kenneth. *The New Industrial State.* Boston: Houghton Mifflin, 1967.

Miller, Herman P. *Income Distribution in the United States.* U. S. Bureau of the Census. Washington: Government Printing Office, 1900.

Myrdal, Gunnar. *Challenge to Affluence.* New York: Pantheon Press, 1963.

Nossiter, Bernard D. *The Mythmakers.* Boston: Houghton Mifflin, 1964.

Orshansky, Mollie. "Who Was Poor in 1966?" *Research and Statistics Note.* Washington: U. S. Department of Health, Education and Welfare (December 6, 1967).

Ward, Barbara. *Spaceship Earth.* New York: Columbia University Press, 1966.

Wogaman, Philip. *Guaranteed Annual Income: The Moral Issues.* Nashville: Abingdon Press, 1968.

11. THE NEW RURAL AMERICA

BASIC TREND

The agriculturally oriented rural community of yesterday is being supplanted by a new community that is rural in terms of appearance, population, density, and scale, but that has a strong urban orientation in terms of employment, culture, values, and communication.

The most highly visible evidence of this trend is the decline of agriculture as a factor in the American economy. While the 3.2 million farms valued at $273,000,000,000 still constituted the largest single industry in the United States in 1968, agriculture no longer dominates the life of the nation.

In 1900 farm workers numbered 10.9 million and accounted for 37 percent of the total labor force. In 1966 there were 3.9 million farm workers, and they represented 5.1 percent of the nation's labor force—compared to 7.4 million or 11.7 percent as recently as 1950. A dramatic illustration of what has happened is that between 1961 and 1967 the annual demand for harvest farm labor in the Mississippi Delta dropped from 750,000 man days to 95,000 man days.

There has been a comparable decrease in the farm population. The total number of Americans living on farms hovered around the 30 million level from the turn of the century through 1940, and the 1935 total of 32.2 million was slightly above the earlier peak of 32 million in 1920. During the World War II period this total dropped to about 24 million and then leveled off at that point for a half dozen years. During the 1950's and 1960's, however, there has been a continued decrease as people moved away from the farm. In 1953 alone, over two million people moved off the farm, and this migration from the farm passed the million mark in three different years during the 1960's. From April, 1966 to April, 1967 the farm population decreased by over 700,000 according to the Bureau of the Census. By 1968 the farm population had dropped to slightly less than 11 million. In percentage terms the decline in the farm population has been even more dramatic. In 1920 one person in three in this nation lived on a farm. Forty-eight years later the proportion was one in 20.

Two characteristics of this change in the number of persons living on farms merit special attention here. The first is the sharp decline in the 25 to 44 age group. Their number dropped from 3.2 million in 1960 to 2.2 million in 1966. One result was that while in 1960 the 25-44 age group and the 55-64 age bracket each accounted for 9 percent of the total farm population, by 1966 the proportion age 25-44 had fallen to 7.8 percent while those age 55-64 had risen to 11.4 percent (and those age 65 and over rose from 8.5 percent to 10.2 percent). Another result of this change is that while in 1950 the number of births in farm families exceeded the number of deaths by 392,000, in 1966 this difference was only 90,000.

The other important consideration is that by 1968 the pro-

portion of farm residents employed in nonagricultural occupations had risen sharply, especially in the South. In 1960
one-third of the employed farm residents were employed
solely or primarily in nonagricultural jobs; by 1968 this
proportion had risen to two-fifths for the nation as a whole
and to nearly 50 percent in the South.

A second important basic trend was mentioned briefly in
Chapter 1 and is a product of the basic urge in millions of
Americans to escape the city. This can be seen most clearly
in the preferences of three groups—the wealthy, the retired,
and the vacationer. All three groups display a strong desire
to go from the crowded urban community to the sparsely
populated rural community.

While the definition of "urban" repeatedly has been
amended to be more inclusive—one result is that thousands
of Americans change from the rural to urban category without moving—the rural population of the nation has hovered
around the 50 to 60 million figure since 1910. Thus while the
percentage of the population living in urban areas has risen
dramatically, and while the actual number of persons living
on farms has dropped by two-thirds, the total rural population has remained relatively constant. This means a sharp
increase in the *rural nonfarm* population has occurred. From
1930 to 1968 the *urban* population of the nation more than
doubled in numbers—from 69 million to 145 million. During
the same period, however, the rural *nonfarm* population
also more than doubled from 24 million in 1930 to over 55
million in 1968 (for reasons of consistency both figures are
based on the 1940 definition of urban and rural).

It is important to recognize this is more than simply a
demographic curiosity. This sharp growth in the rural nonfarm population is the product of several forces. These include the development of a freeway network linking rural
communities to the heart of the large cities, widespread own-

ership of the automobile, a reduction in the length of the work week between 1900 and 1960, environmental pollution in the cities, school consolidation in rural areas, a shift in public policy on taxation and financing governmental services in the direction of collecting revenues on the basis of wealth and distributing on the basis of need, the migration of Negroes to the large cities and racial prejudice, the rise in the levels of personal income, and the decentralization of industry.

Finally, the impact of the United States Department of Agriculture (U.S.D.A.) on this general trend merits attention. For decades the primary responsibility of the U.S.D.A. was to help the farmer improve his techniques and obtain a better price for his products. Gradually, however, the Department began to place more emphasis on helping all members of the farm family reach a better living level. This was then broadened to include all rural people, both farm and nonfarm. Today the U.S.D.A. is organized to serve *all* the residents of *all* the communities, regardless of population size, located in any of the 2,500 counties that are outside a standard metropolitan statistical area *and* also many of the residents of metropolitan counties.

Today the U.S.D.A. has extensive programs directed to the economic development of rural America, to the rebuilding and revitalization of thousands of villages and small cities, to the improvement of housing and public facilities in rural communities, and to the general decentralization of the population.

If achieved, the goal articulated by the U.S.D.A. is one that will transform rural America. "Imagine, if you will, a time in the future when the American landscape is dotted with communities that include a blend of renewed small cities, new towns, and growing rural villages. Each is a cluster with its own jobs and industries; its own college or university; its own medical center; its own cultural, entertainment, and recreational centers; and with an agriculture fully sharing in the national prosperity.

"Imagine hundreds of such communities that would make it possible for 300 million Americans to live in less congestion than 200 million live today—that would enable urban centers to become free of smog and blight, free of overcrowding, with ample parkland within easy reach of all." *

IMPLICATIONS

In general terms these changes in rural America mean the churches and denominations should take a new look at their traditional attitudes and policies. In more specific terms a half dozen points can be lifted up for immediate attention.

1. It now appears that much, perhaps all, of the *increase* in population in the United States between 1965 and 1985 will be accommodated in what were essentially rural communities in 1965.

Some of these rural communities are located within metropolitan counties and will be assimilated into the expanding metropolitan complex as urbanized areas. The residents living in these rural communities will become "urbanized" without ever changing their address. This is simply a continuation of a pattern that prevailed from 1945 to 1965.

During this last round of the urbanization of the rural fringe thousands of rural churches went through some interesting experiences. For some, these experiences were creative. For others, they were traumatic. The lessons that

---

* (From *Communities of Tomorrow* published by the U. S. Department of Agriculture.)

were learned from those experiences should be collected, analyzed, and made available to the people in the rural churches that are about to experience similar (but not identical) changes.

Many of the rural communities in which much of this population growth will be accommodated are located in counties outside existing metropolitan areas. Some of these counties will be added to existing or newly created standard metropolitan areas in the traditional sense of the word. For a variety of reasons, however, distance and area being the two most obvious, most of these counties will not be urbanized in the traditional manner.

Instead of the line of urbanization moving out to engulf most of the land in these counties, a more selective process will occur. Here and there in these counties existing villages and cities will experience a population boom. In other places new towns will be developed. Between these urbanized clusters will be large areas of open space. This pattern of dispersed urbanization will spread out to perhaps 60 to 100 miles from the nearest large city. To the observer flying over these urbanizing counties they will appear to be overwhelmingly rural with a scattering of urban clusters. The clusters will be linked by high-speed transportation arteries.

Basically this is a new form of urbanization. In a typical county this may mean the community that had 500 residents in 1965 will have 10,000 in 1985; or the one with a population of 3,500 in 1965 may grow to 25,000 by 1985. Some will be largely residential. In others the number of jobs will greatly outnumber the size of the resident labor force. Some will be the site of a college or university. Others will have factories or research centers, and many will have an economic base built around a few large offices, perhaps the headquarters for a large national corporation.

For the three or six or sixteen churches that existed in these communities in 1965 this will be a challenging experience. They will find the shock of change more difficult to respond to than the apparent opportunities for growth. They will be disturbed as new congregations are organized in what will appear to be a very competitive manner by the "noncooperative" branches of American Protestantism. They will be torn between the resource-consuming demand for their own institutional adjustments and the call to be engaged in the process of change in the community outside the church doors.

2. A second obvious consequence of this trend will be felt by the town and country movement. This has been an extremely strong force in American Protestantism. On the one hand it will be challenged to new responses by this new trend. On the other hand it will be threatened by those who contend that the movement should disband or be absorbed in some structure because it was developed on a set of circumstances that no longer prevail. Will the town and country movement be able to change its orientation and its role? Will it be absorbed by a newer concept that discards the rural-urban dichotomy in favor of a church-community-change concept?

3. By 1985 this new trend will be felt in perhaps 1,000 counties that were labeled rural in 1965. Some of these will be added to the approximately 600 counties that constituted the metropolitan areas of the nation in 1965. Most of the 1,000, however, will be in this new rural-urban category well outside existing metropolitan centers. This leaves approximately 1,500 counties in which the pattern will continue to be one of an aging population decreasing in numbers as economic opportunities diminish. In these counties the local churches have been and will continue to be faced by difficult problems. On the one hand their institutional

strength declines with the decrease in population. On the other hand they function in communities that tend to have the fewest public service, the fewest staffed voluntary agencies, the lowest level of community resources, and the greatest per capita needs.

These same counties tend to have the most churches per 1,000 members, the fewest members per congregation, the parishes with the least resources to fill the void and meet the needs of the community, and the fewest and weakest councils of churches. In Vinton County, Ohio, for example, there are 25 United Methodist, United Church of Christ, Episcopal, United Presbyterian, or Christian congregations, or one per 410 residents with an average of 68 members per congregation. In Summit County, which includes the city of Akron, the comparable figures for these five denominations are 124 congregations or one per 4,200 residents and an average of 640 members per congregation.

There is a serious risk that in the effort to help the churches in the other 1,600 counties respond to the more highly visible changes described earlier, the problems of the churches in these 1,000 to 1,500 declining rural counties may be overlooked.

4. Much of the effort to implement the desire and demand for interchurch cooperation in the United States has been channeled to councils of churches. Some have been or ganized on a statewide basis, others on a city or metropolitan basis.

How will the counciliar movement relate to this new pattern of growth?

The handicaps of size, distance and identity will make it difficult for each of these rural-urban counties to have a separate council. It will be even more difficult for an existing metropolitan council to serve areas 40 or 50 or 60 or 100 miles away. Very few metropolitan councils in a metropolitan area embracing two or three or four or five counties have been effective outside the central county. Does this new pattern suggest development of regional councils? Or should there be a council of councils?

5. This decentralization trend may tend to increase the already severe problem of the compartmentalization of the population along economic, racial, ethnic, educational, social, and cultural lines (see Chapter 12). While it is possible that many of these "communities of tomorrow" will have considerable economic, educational, and social diversity, the geographical separation, the pressure for a distinctive identity, and the desire to escape the problems of the large city may promote a new degree of parochialism.

During the 1960's the mounting urban crisis made many suburbanites conscious of their interest in the problems of the central city. This new form of the dispersal of the population may re-create the problem. This would make more important and more difficult the reconciling role of the churches.

6. While it is too early to speak with assurance, this new trend appears to be enlarging the role of county government. The county has been the traditional unit of local government through which the U.S.D.A. has channeled its programs. The county is taking on new functions and is expanding in size and importance. (Between 1955 and 1965 the number of full-time employees in municipal government increased by 31 percent; the increase in county government was 48 percent.) In many rural-turning-urban areas the county is providing a range of services that formerly was thought of as the responsibility of a municipality.

Churchmen need to evaluate this trend. For some this means becoming familiar with a unit and form of government that has been neglected by both preachers and political scientists. For others it means the county government of tomorrow will be radically different from the county government they worked with yesterday.

SUGGESTIONS FOR FURTHER READING

Department of Agriculture. *Communities of Tomorrow.* Washington: Government Printing Office, 1967.

Berry, Brian J. L. *Strategies, Models, and Economic Theories of Development in Rural Regions.* Washington: U. S. Department of Agriculture, 1967.

Greene, Shirley. *Ferment on the Fringe: Studies of Rural Churches in Transition.* Philadelphia: Christian Education Press, 1960.

Judy, Marvin. *The Cooperative Parish in Nonmetropolitan Areas.* Nashville: Abingdon Press, 1967.

Schaller, Lyle E. *The Local Church Looks to the Future.* Nashville: Abingdon Press, 1968.

Sills, Horace S. (ed.). *Grassroots Ecumenicity.* Philadelphia: United Church Press, 1967.

12. THE COMPARTMENTALIZATION OF THE POPULATION

BASIC TREND

The population of the United States increasingly is being divided among geographically separated homogeneous compartments.

One of the most important and far-reaching trends of the twentieth century is the division of the population along lines that reflect religion, age, education, marital status, income, wealth, race, culture, ethnic background, language, and social position, *and the increasing geographical separation of these groupings.*

This trend is a product of several factors: the urbanization of the population; the natural tendency of some people to stay close to others of similar origins, backgrounds, or with similar values; the patterns of prejudice and discrimination that have been present in American society for centuries; the preference of some land developers, voters, build-

160

ers, local government officials, and financiers for producing and maintaining homogeneous neighborhoods; the recent geographical dispersal of the urban population (see Chapter 1); and the change from a melting pot practice of assimilation to a concept of pluralism.

There are six dimensions to this trend that merit the attention of contemporary churchmen.

1. In rural America social class distinctions were an important, but not highly visible, part of life. The wealthiest family in town was personally known by many, perhaps by all, of the poorest families in the community. The individual with the highest level of formal education might live in the same block with persons who had not completed the sixth grade.

In today's large cities social class distinctions also are present—but they are intensified by a geographical compartmentalization of the population that greatly reduces person-to-person contacts across social class lines. This lack of person-to-person contacts across social class lines may be the greatest single source of tensions that plague so many of our large cities.

A simple, but somewhat extreme, example of this geographical compartmentalization of the population can be seen in the central city-suburban division in Cuyahoga County (Ohio).

A continuation of recent trends—and there is every reason to believe these trends will continue unless the attractiveness of housing in Cleveland improves—suggests that in 1970 the population of Cleveland will include 435,000 whites and 305,000 Negroes. It now appears probable that in 1970 suburban Cuyahoga County will include 60 percent of the residents of the County, 90 percent of the college graduates of the County (age 25 and over), 90 percent of the families with an annual income of $15,000 or more and 97 percent of the families in the over-$25,000 income bracket, 14 percent of the Negro population, 80 percent of the white population affiliated with the mainline Protestant churches, 99.7 percent of the Jewish population of the County, 20 percent of the unemployed residents of the County, 20 percent of the substandard housing, 0 percent of the public housing, 25 percent of the families with an income below the 1970 "poverty line," 8 percent of the ADC (Aid to Dependent Children) families, and 10 percent of the relief cases in the County.

A similar pattern can be detected in literally scores of other metropolitan areas.

2. A second extremely important dimension of this trend is related to the decentralization trend described in Chapter 1 and the migration patterns described in Chapter 7. This is the physical separation of the persons in the 18-24 age group from the older generations. The largest group of immigrants to most central cities are persons in the 18-24 age group. They are attracted by educational, vocational, and marital opportunities.

This physical separation of the generations cannot help intensifying the problems of communication and understanding that long have been inherent in the generation gap.

3. The homogeneity of the residents in any one of these compartments is being reinforced as people divide—and are divided—along racial, age, and income lines. Thus there is a tendency not only to concentrate elderly people in one place, but also to further divide the elderly along racial and economic lines.

This has produced one neighborhood composed of low income elderly Negroes, another composed of low income elderly Caucasians, a third composed of middle and upper income elderly whites, and so forth.

Some of the recent well-intentioned efforts to help the

less fortunate have intensified this problem, the most highly visible illustration of this being church-sponsored housing projects for the elderly.

The fact that in 1966, for example, families headed by a person over 65 or under 25 accounted for only 7 percent of all high income households, and 40 percent of all low income households should serve as a warning to those well meaning people who by their proposed "good deeds" would further intensify the compartmentalization of the population along age and income lines.

A 1968 study by the University of Chicago's Pritzker School of Medicine and the Committee on Human Development revealed that 24 percent of the persons who entered homes for the aged died within six months while only 10 percent of those on the waiting list, but still living within a community setting, died during that same period of time.

4. In Chapter 10 it was pointed out that the accumulated wealth of the nation increasingly is owned by corporations, pension funds, foundations, and other organizations rather than by individuals. This means that the people who control the use of this wealth have more restrictions placed on them than applied to the individual who had accumulated or inherited a personal fortune.

Combine this change with the trend toward the increased geographical and social separation of these managers of wealth from those militant indigenous leaders of the poor who are articulating strongly held ideas on how this wealth should be used, and it is easy to see why alienation is growing, tension is increasing, and protests are becoming more visible. One inevitable result of this that is already beginning to appear is to move the location of the protest action from the neighborhood of the poor to the neighborhood of the managers of wealth.

5. Many of the recent newcomers to the central cities and

older suburban communities come from a different subculture than that of the previous residents. In the late nineteenth and early twentieth centuries many of the newcomers to the central cities came from Europe with a highly visible and different cultural heritage. Today most of the newcomers come from the same general culture, but from different subcultures. The differences in language, customs, religious beliefs, and dress are very important, but not as highly visible as formerly. Even more important are differences in value systems, educational attainment, social class, race, religious culture, and income levels. Since these have a lower degree of visibility people are not as conscious of the need to recognize, honor, and accept these differences.

6. A countertrend is at work. One facet of this is the rapid increase in the size of the middle class described in Chapter 9. There is no question but that the separation along ethnic, language, cultural and to a certain extent along racial lines, is not as sharp as it was a decade ago and that this trend is continuing. On the other hand this trend is tending to reinforce the geographical compartmentalization along the lines of age, wealth, income, marital status, social position, and education.

IMPLICATIONS

The implications of this trend for the parish are very challenging.

1. Perhaps the greatest challenge is to acknowledge openly this trend and to study the implications for the parish. This is especially challenging for the parish that reflects this compartmentalization in its membership. Does this mean there is a special call to such a congregation to place an unusually heavy emphasis on a ministry of reconciliation?

Or does this mean that there is a special call to such a parish to lead in reducing the extent of this geographical separation?

2. This trend also raises difficult questions for those who have consistently endorsed and supported the concept of the geographical parish. When the creation or continuation of a parish with clearly defined geographical boundaries also means drawing most of the members from such a homogeneous compartment, should the concept of the geographical parish be scrapped? Or should the ministry of that parish be broadened to overcome the limitations suggested by the expression that "our membership reflects the neighborhood in which the building is located"? At what point does this become the equivalent of abandoning the concept of the geographical parish?

3. The shift from differences along cultural lines to less visible distinctions based on subculture raises questions for the parish, the denomination, and the interchurch agencies.

When the cultural differences were great the Christian gospel was preached within the context of each culture, and the cultural differences were recognized. Today when the differences in the subcultures are less visible, little attempt is made to provide a ministry within the context of the subculture of the newcomer—and one result is that most of the newcomers are not reached by the churches in the larger denominations from the mainstream of American Protestantism.

For a congregation this raises important questions in terms of evangelism, outreach, and the assimilation of newcomers. Too many congregations have decided to relocate, merge, or disband rather than to respond to the challenge of ministering to people from a different subculture.

For a denomination this means new responsibilities in helping parishes adapt. It means the establishment of new ministries in old neighborhoods. It means new expressions of cooperation. For a Council of Churches it means affirmative efforts to broaden its constituency. It may also mean new efforts in research and planning to help the congretions and denominations respond to their obligations.

4. For those who seek to represent the prophetic voice of the church and for those who seek to reverse this trend challenging questions also are raised.

For example, in recent years some churchmen have developed and articulated the goal of creating neighborhoods that are racially and economically heterogeneous. Their efforts have been discouraged by sociologists, educators, and students of family life who agree that a racially mixed neighborhood poses no serious problems; but who argue that mixing families of widely varying incomes in the same block or neighborhood produces tensions that many low and low middle income families cannot cope with. What is the appropriate goal for the person who cannot accept this, but who is apprehensive about impairing the family life of any income group?

5. This trend also supplies a yardstick for evaluating new parish and denominational programs. Will this proposal accentuate or increase this geographical compartmentalization? Or will it decrease it? Or is this group not concerned with this standard for evaluation?

6. Perhaps most important, an awareness of this trend helps explain why the problems of race and poverty were able to be kept from view for so long before they were recognized as national scandals. One reason was that many people who held the power to change conditions were geographically removed from the location of the problem and thus did not see the seriousness of these conditions.

This raises a very critical question. What other problems

are being concealed by the growing compartmentalization of the population?

SUGGESTIONS FOR FURTHER READING

Glazer, Nathan and Moynihan, Daniel P. *Beyond the Melting Pot.* Cambridge: M.I.T. Press, 1963.

Gordon, Milton. *Assimilation in American Life.* New York: Oxford University Press, 1964.

Lenski, Gerhard. *The Religious Factor.* Garden City, N.Y.: Doubleday, 1961.

Von Eckardt, Wolf. *A Place To Live.* New York: Delacorte Press, 1967.

13. ALIENATION AND PROTEST

BASIC TREND

The alienation of the individual from the structures and institutions of society will continue to become more pronounced, more visible, and more widespread.

One of the most important trends of the last third of the twentieth century is the growing sense of alienation felt and expressed by an apparently rapidly growing number of people in the United States.

This trend has such a high degree of visibility—it probably is more visible than any other trend identified in this book—that it is not necessary to document its existence. Before looking at some of the implications for the churches, however, it may be helpful to lift up for a brief examination a couple of the causes and characteristics of this trend and to offer a few interpretations.

1. To a substantial degree this is a rebellion, especially by sensitive young persons, against a society that is increasing-

ly object-oriented. It is also a rebellion against the depersonalization of the individual in a mass society.

Signs of this rebellion against a depersonalized and object-oriented society can be seen in the favorable response to the establishment of the Peace Corps, which within four years after it was established had a larger number of people at work abroad than did all the American churches combined.

Signs of this rebellion against a depersonalized and object-oriented society also can be seen in the attacks on the "multiversity," in the current wave of anti-church-building sentiment, in some of the anti-draft movements, in the difficulty many large corporations have had in their programs to recruit college seniors, in the response of a majority of suburbanites to proposals for metropolitan government, and in recent strong support by officials in Washington to decentralize the operations of the federal government.

Another example to illustrate the point that this has become an object-oriented society can be seen in the long series of proposals to solve the housing problem for low income families by technological improvements in the home building industry rather than by facing directly the problem of enabling low income families to move up the income ladder. Here and in other areas the benefits of innovation have been directed largely at objects rather than at people.

2. It is impossible to understand this trend or to speculate about the implications of it unless it is recognized that the current wave of rebels and protestors includes a mixture of reformers and revolutionaries. There is a vast difference between the person who feels alienated from what he believes to be an unjust society and sets out on a course aimed at reforming that society and the individual who has a similar sense of alienation and sets out to destroy the institutions and structures of that society. Whether the causes

of these differences are political, psychological, economic, or emotional is a question beyond this discussion. The crucial point is to recognize that the leadership of this wave of protests does include these two very different types.

3. Closely related to this point is the fact that as the degree of alienation from society increases, the easier and more tempting it is to turn from being a reformer to becoming a nihilist or an anarchist or a revolutionary.

4. One of the most frequently stated criticisms of the current wave of protests is that the protesters do not appear to have a substitute in mind for that which they seek to destroy. They often appear to be nihilists rather than reformers. They can define grievances and point to injustices but rarely can they offer solutions.

Such a criticism reveals a failure to distinguish among the nihilists, the reformers, and the revolutionaries on the New Left. It also reflects a failure to understand the spirit of the true revolutionary. Rebels against society who are in fact reformers normally have a reasonably clear objective in mind, and they expect to achieve that objective within the basic framework of existing institutions and structures.

An excellent example of this was the dynamic civil rights leader of the early 1960's who led the protests against racial injustice, but who believed that racial justice and the racial integration of the society could be achieved within the context of the existing institutions and structures of society. He argued that these institutions and structures needed reforming, but he believed they could be reformed.

The rebel who is actually a revolutionary usually seeks only to express the spirit of rebellion. This type of rebel normally does not feel constrained to offer any positive alternatives. Revolutionaries normally do not feel compelled to offer "replacement" programs. Their goal is to destroy what they believe is no longer tolerable. Philosophically they accept the Maoist doctrine that "before you can build you must destroy."

An example of this was the militant protester of the late 1960's who had concluded that justice and peace could not be obtained by simply reforming the structures and institutions of American society. He felt constrained to destroy these institutions and structures since they could not be reformed.

These differences between the reformer and the revolutionary must be recognized by anyone seeking to understand the current wave of alienation and protest. The reformer strongly believes such historic rights as the right of free speech and the right of peaceful assembly must be protected for *everyone*. The revolutionary regards this as an irrelevant consideration since all the institutions and structures of society, including these rights, will be destroyed in the revolution that must occur before a new society can be built. The reformer believes the rules are changed by following the rulebook. The revolutionary sees the rulebook as only one of the resources to be used in bringing on the revolution that will result in burning the rulebook. The reformer expects to achieve his goal through such means as confrontation, nonviolent conflict, debate, and elections. The revolutionary believes that confrontation, debate, and elections will not be adequate tools for achieving his goal and expects to move on to the use of violence, arson, and weapons.

5. Another very important part of this total picture that often is overlooked because of the high visibility of the protest movements is that this sense of alienation is not confined to the young or to the poor or to the participants in the peace movements or to those involved in the struggle for racial justice.

This growing sense of alienation among the American

people can be seen in modern art, in contemporary poetry and fiction, in the churches, in the clergy, in the affluent suburbs, in the ghetto, in politics, among the hippies, in the professional and graduate schools, and in the large corporation, and on the farm.

Those who seek to explain what is happening and why often point to the erosion of the work-oriented, advance-oriented, and achievement-oriented system of values that undergirded American society for decades. In what is sometimes labelled a "post-industrial society" there is a growing rejection of the goal of wealth for wealth's sake, of the older achievement-oriented goals, and of what is sometimes described as the "rat race" that involves so many adults.

A new emphasis is beginning to emerge that places a higher premium on interpersonal relationships than on vocational advancement, on the power of love than on the power of wealth, on human dignity than on social or professional status. There is an increasing emphasis on meaning and purpose as it becomes easier to "make a living" and to survive the old stark life and death struggles.

Among other consequences this suggests that a major change in the American system may be taking place. Persons born before the second World War were reared in a culture that inculcated a system of values that may now be in the process of being replaced by a new system that places a greater emphasis on persons rather than material possessions or on economic or social status. Older persons are caught in this transition, and their difficulties are intensified by the emergence of a highly articulate younger generation that is attacking the old set of values while also endorsing the new set and attempting to hasten the pace of the transition.

The difficulties the rational person has in comprehending

and accepting this are multiplied by the many exceptions to this generalization that he sees all around among persons of all ages.

An excellent illustration of the problems of communication produced by differences in age and perspective occurred in the 1968 presidential campaign when young adults were urged to (a) become involved and (b) abstain from voting.

6. It is impossible to predict how long it will take for the current wave of alienation and protest to institutionalize a new set of values in American society. It also is impossible to predict whether the current wave of protests will produce the desired reforms or spark a revolution—and there are many who contend that the United States is closer to revolution than at any time since 1932. It does appear safe to predict, however, that this wave of alienation will widen and that the protest movements will grow in number, variety, and scope.

By the latter part of 1968 this wave of protests had broadened out far beyond the peace movement, the struggle for equal participation by the black man, and the efforts to eliminate poverty and improve the lot of the poor and the underprivileged. This sense of alienation and the several waves of protest had engulfed institutions of higher education, the political scene, the scholarly professional societies, the white churches and the black churches, the military establishment, and organized labor.

It appears that this trend will broaden and in the next few years engulf many other institutions including the Roman Catholic Church, the American Medical Association, the large corporation, the seminaries, the voluntary social and welfare organizations, and every other institution that has built a wall between the institution or the management of the institution and its clientele.

IMPLICATIONS

Again the prominence of this trend and the limitations of space make it unrealistic to attempt to do any more than to identify an illustrative assortment of the implications of this trend.

1. Unquestionably the most important implication of this trend for the churches is that many, but not all, of the youthful protesters of the New Left are articulating ideals, desires, and goals that represent a combination of the best elements of the United States Constitution, the gospel of Jesus Christ, and the proclamations of the prophets of the Old Testament.

This is difficult for many devoted churchmen to comprehend, because they see more than they hear. Instead of hearing the cry for social justice *now,* they often see what they identify as the arrogance of youth. Instead of hearing the call for self-sacrifice, they see what appears to be a selfish and self-centered struggle for power. Instead of hearing the plea for brotherhood, they see a militant attack on the customary ways of carrying out the responsibilities of the organization and of effecting change. This means the parish has an extremely urgent and very difficult task of interpretation as it seeks to help the person over thirty comprehend what is happening and why.

2. Closely related to this is another very critical implication. For the person in the local church this is a trend that he cannot ignore. He must respond. This means he must make choices.

What is his general response to this trend? To support a repression of protest and a harsh "law and order" response to the militant protesters? Or will he sense there is another alternative—opening the doors for new opportunities for greater involvement "in the system"?

While it usually is difficult to support the contention that any problem has only an "either-or" type of solution, this may be one of those rare occasions when society actually is confronted with only an either-or choice. Perhaps the only choices are either greater involvement by the alienated or repression of those who express their alienation by protest, by apathy, or by adopting nonconventional forms of dress and behavior.

Closely related to this is another choice. Reform or revolution? It should be emphasized here that there are many dedicated Christians who have concluded there is no hope for achieving peace and social justice except by destroying the existing institutions and structures of American society and building a new social order from a fresh start.

The overwhelming majority of American churchmen probably cannot comprehend such a conclusion, much less accept or support it. For them this raises a new question: What is the best way to prevent a revolution? By repression? By moving toward creation of a police state? Or by opening up new opportunities for meaningful participation by the protester, the apathetic, and the alienated?

3. While most of the discussion in both this chapter and the wider public arena limit the basic alternatives to reform or revolution, there may be a third choice.

In a provocative book *Landmarks of Tomorrow* Peter Drucker has suggested a third method of effecting change. He contends that innovation is neither reform nor revolution and that the goal of innovation is to create something new without either the disruptive effects of revolution or the break with tradition that usually is a part of any reform movement.

Those churchmen who are repelled by both revolution and by reform as they understand it, but who recognize the necessity of making choices and the need for affirmative action, might consider this alternative.

4. One of the consequences of the current wave of alienation and protest that is of grave concern to all Christians is the rise in the level of hatred in the nation. There are many adults who hate young people. One impact of this generation gap on the local church was revealed by a survey of church members on Cleveland's west side. Residents in this all-white section of Cleveland traditionally have displayed great hostility toward Negroes, public housing, and open housing. The survey sought to discover the areas in which they believed their churches should be *less* active. In second, third, and fourth place among the responses (58 percent of the respondents were age 45 or older) were: supporting more liberal welfare legislation, the implementation of the state open housing law, and securing more public housing (which presumably would bring low income Negroes to the west side). In first place was operating a coffeehouse for young people. In the 1968 presidential campaigns there were Democrats who expressed a definite hatred of Hubert Humphrey, and there were Republicans who articulated a hatred for Richard Nixon. There are many whites who hate Negroes, and there are many black people who hate white folks. There are many middle and upper income persons who hate the poor, and there are poor who hate the wealthy. Residents of the central city hate the suburbanites and vice versa.

The churches have an obligation to speak to this condition.

5. One of the products of this increasing sense of alienation, of the frustration produced by either-or choices, of the rise in the level of hate, and of the gap between the haves and the have-nots is an increasingly receptive climate for an authoritarian figure to step forth and offer to settle all these problems if the people will but entrust this responsibility to him.

At the same time that there is a general trend toward the

decentralization of power and an increase in the power of self-determination, there also appears to be a growing number of people who would welcome or at least accept an authoritarian political regime both locally and nationally.

Here again the prophetic voice of the parish, and the denomination cannot afford to be silent. If they wait too long they may forfeit both the right and the freedom to speak.

6. As a part of the reconciling ministry of the church the parish might consider systematic efforts to help people understand the other side. In addition to the usual exhortation on the subject, it might be helpful to program study classes. For example, a parish might develop a study course on the writings of Herbert Marcuse, who often has been referred to as the philosopher of the current protest movement —and he also has been labeled by *Pravda* as "an agent of the CIA."

Adult churchmen cannot expect to respond effectively to the trends identified in this chapter without doing their homework. The parish can help them do their homework.

7. In general terms, this trend challenges the parish to a ministry of reconciliation that includes listening, study, interpretation, confrontation, and communication.

In addition to this ministry, which in most parishes will be directed largely at the members of the congregation, there is another, more active role for the parish. This is the ministry of change—of changing the attitudes of people, of helping reform the structures of society, and of social innovation. This is a ministry aimed at enlarging the old opportunities and opening up new opportunities for meaningful participation by all people of all ages without regard to color. A part of this ministry of change can be carried out unilaterally by the parish. Part of it requires the cooperation of the parish with other parishes and with the other forms of the church.

8. Finally there is the challenge to the parish to be a moral force in the community. The church must speak to the causes of this wave of alienation and protest. It must not be hesitant on calling for change where change is needed and in helping to effect change.

In addition the churches, and in terms of effectiveness this usually means the parish church, must speak to the moral issues. It must help people draw the line between violence and dissent, between civil disobedience and intentional provocation, between legitimate expressions of dissent and illegitimate efforts to dramatize dissent, between illegality and immorality, and between proper moral objections and the ignoring of the rights of others. Most of all, the churches must speak to the moral issue involved when the end is used to justify the means.

SUGGESTIONS FOR FURTHER READING

Arnold, O. Carroll. "Fight Fiercely, Christians," *The Christian Century* (June 19, 1968).

Blauner, Robert. *Alienation and Freedom: The Factory Worker and His Industry.* Chicago: University of Chicago Press, 1964.

Daedalus. This entire issue was devoted to "Students and Politics." (Winter, 1968.)

Drucker, Peter. *Landmarks of Tomorrow.* New York: Harper, 1959.

Erikson, Eric H. *Identity: Youth and Crisis.* New York: W. W. Norton, 1968.

Fortas, Abe. *Concerning Dissent and Civil Disobedience.* New York: New American Library, 1968.

Jencks, Christopher and Riesman, David. *The Academic Revolution.* Garden City, N.Y.: Doubleday, 1968.

The Journal of Social Issues. (This entire issue was devoted to "Stirrings Out of Apathy: Student Activism and the Decade of Protest.") XXIII, 3 (July 1967).

Kelman, Steven. "The Feud Among the Radicals." *Harper's Magazine* (June, 1966).

———. "Beyond New Leftism." *Commentary* (February, 1969).

Marcuse, Herbert. *One-Dimensional Man*. Boston: Beacon Press, 1964.

———. *Reason and Revolution*. Boston: Beacon Press, 1954.

Michael, Donald N. *The Next Generation*. New York: Vintage Books, 1965.

PART FOUR

CHANGES IN THE SOURCE AND DISTRIBUTION OF POWER

14. THE DEMAND FOR SELF-DETERMINATION

BASIC TREND

The worldwide surge for power to control one's own destiny is being expressed in all segments of society and will continue to expand.

The drive for the power of self-determination is one of the two or three most important worldwide trends of the last half of the twentieth century. It first became highly visible after World War II as literally scores of former colonies sought and gained their independence. It appeared in the United States in the struggle for racial justice, first in the fight for racial integration and later in the black man's demand that he be allowed to set his own goals.

It attained an even higher degree of visibility as students battled for the right to have a voice in the policy-making process at the institutions they attended, in the founding of "free universities," and in the development that found students setting up and administering courses within the curriculum of hundreds of colleges and universities.

The same trend was both reflected and strengthened in the concept of the "maximum feasible participation of the residents" that was written into the original anti-poverty legislation adopted by Congress in 1964.

It reached the stage of a worldwide debate in 1968 when Roman Catholic theologians seriously supported the view that the man and wife, not the Pope, should determine whether a Catholic couple were free to choose what form of birth control technique they would use.

It was reflected in the sudden increase in the number of Roman Catholic clergy who left the priesthood. The monthly average in the United States rose from 20 in 1966 to 40 in 1967 to over 50 in 1968. Well over one-third of these ex-priests married soon after leaving the priesthood.

This same trend also was reflected in professional sports where, after decades of leaving such matters to the club owners, the athletes and officials began to organize and demand a voice in the determination of their working conditions and their compensation.

Many other examples could be cited to illustrate the growth of this trend, a trend that might be described more accurately as a worldwide movement.

Before looking at some of the implications for the churches it might be helpful to examine a few of the more general effects and consequences of this trend.

1. Regardless of the organization or institution one consequence of this trend is that it now is necessary to bring more people into the process earlier. Whether the process is goal formulation, the development of a statement of purpose, the reorganization of an existing agency, or a change in the arrangement of desks in a large office, today the people affected by these decisions want a voice in making the

decision. The primary emphasis in the problem-solving process must now be on the process, on equal participation, and on the opportunity for involvement, rather than on some idealized solution dreamed up by one or two persons.

2. Instead of discouraging participation and suppressing dissent, this new trend makes it desirable and often necessary to encourage broader involvement and to deal more openly with dissent. This is threatening to many people and often produces a new set of tensions that can be very disruptive.

3. The demand for self-determination often stands in direct opposition to the old pattern of vesting control in a hierarchy that had lines of authority running in only one direction.

4. This trend is closely related to the growing sense of alienation identified in the previous chapter. For example, to many young people today the forefeiture of the right of self-determination by a person in the 16 to 25 age bracket is an act with more serious consequences than civil disobedience, vandalism, violence, or open rebellion. This is very difficult for the older adult, who has accepted both social and self-imposed restrictions on his own behavior, to understand.

5. One of the major conflicts produced by this trend is that more people are caught up in the dilemma of choosing between immediate or short-term desires and long-term goals. The 16 year old demands the right to decide whether to remain in school or drop out. He wants to make the choice between the attractions of a job and income now or staying in school and being dependent on an allowance from his parents. The leaders of the new nation in South America or Africa have to choose between increasing the supply of consumer goods now or using these resources to build up the capital plant of the country.

These and similar decisions are now being made by people operating from a different set of values than guided those who had the authority and responsibility for making similar decisions 20 years ago.

IMPLICATIONS

1. For the decision makers in the parish an awareness of this trend should encourage them to re-examine the way policy is developed and decisions are made in their local church. Are the people who will be affected involved in this process?

2. For the parish that has difficulties in "reaching the young people" an awareness of this trend may suggest new alternatives. Instead of planning programs and activities that, hopefully, will "attract" these young people it might be wiser to encourage the participation by young people in both the planning *and the execution* phases of these efforts.

3. For both the parish and the denominational judicatory this trend suggests the need for developing new means of handling the internal conflict that is produced by this new emphasis on self-determination. Stanley Hallet suggests that instead of attempting to suppress conflict, the goal should be to place greater emphasis on the legislative arm of the organization (official board, church council, session, voters' assembly, vestry, presbytery meeting, or annual meeting) as a place where conflict can be expressed and compromises can be worked out in a creative manner.

4. For decades the parish, like most voluntary organizations, has operated on the principle that a consensus is desirable before action is taken. The emergence of this demand for self-determination threatens this old system since now it will be more difficult to achieve a consensus. This

means it may be necessary to help church members accept the principle of majority rule and be willing to subject themselves to the discipline of putting loyalty above self-expression.

5. For the churchman interested in social change this trend also raises a very important question. Can he continue to advocate and support change with the expectation that he and other like-minded people will be able to control the pace and direction of change? Or does this mean that the control over the direction and pace of change usually will be seized by those most affected by the consequences of change?

6. For clergymen, both Catholic and Protestant, the emergence of this "right" of self-determination creates a new set of tensions that can drive many of them out of the ministry. Previously, when it was assumed that they did not have this right but rather were under the discipline of an ecclesiastical superior, they were not confronted with the choices that face them today. The disciplines of the vocation relieved them of the authority—and the responsibility—for making certain decisions. Now they feel they must work out the answers themselves. This cannot help producing serious tensions within the man as he is caught between what he identifies as his vocation and what he regards as his rights as a human being and as a child of God.

This trend will strengthen the drift toward a "connectional" type of church polity (see Chapter 20), especially in those denominations where the pastor is appointed by a higher ecclesiastical authority. This trend means both the pastor and the people in the parish will demand a greater voice in the pastoral placement process.

7. For denominational officials this trend means that it will become increasingly difficult to "hand down" programs to be implemented by the local church.

8. For every Christian, whether he is serving on a committee within the local church or on a hospital board or in public office or simply functioning as a taxpayer and voter this growing demand for the right of self-determination is producing a new concept that he must understand. In simple terms this is a shift in the distribution of power between the "client" and the "system."

The client sees himself as receiving service from a system on a basis in which the nature and the quality of the service and the priorities are determined by the system. The client is now insisting on having a greater voice in the determination of how the system will operate, in deciding on the nature and quality of the product produced by the system, and on the ordering of priorities.

To illustrate this development one can substitute for "system-client" such pairs of words and phrases as college-student, welfare agency-welfare recipient, hospital-patient, factory-worker, church council-church member, denomination-local church, public school-parents and pupils, apartment building owner-tenant, farm price support programs-farmer, and many others.

SUGGESTIONS FOR FURTHER READING

Boulding, Kenneth E. *The Meaning of the Twentieth Century*. New York: Harper, 1964.

Callahan, Daniel. "Revolution in the Cloth," *The Saturday Review* (July 29, 1967).

Ford, Thomas R. (ed.). *The Revolutionary Theme in Contemporary America*. Lexington: University of Kentucky Press, 1967.

Ways, Max. "The Dynamite in Rising Expectations," *Fortune* (May, 1968).

15. KNOWLEDGE AS A SOURCE OF POWER

BASIC TREND

Knowledge is emerging as the most important source of power.

Historically the usual sources of power have been force, land, production facilities, money, love, charisma, organization, the accident of birth, and parents or ancestors.

For centuries man has realized that knowledge could be an important source of power. This was recognized long ago in the expression, "In the land of the blind, the one-eyed man is king." Only recently, however, has knowledge become widely accepted as an extremely important source of power. The twentieth-century "managerial revolution," which has given to expert administrators rather than to the owners control of nearly all the large corporations, is one example of this. The power within the business community of the specialist in corporation law or corporate finance is another example. It was knowledge that enabled

Robert S. McNamara to become the first Secretary of Defense to control the armed forces of the nation.

In nearly every arena where decisions are being made it is the person with the most knowledge about a specialized subject (or the person who has done his homework most thoroughly) who has the greatest power in influencing the decisions. This can be seen when the motorist takes his balky automobile to the garage, when an individual invests money in the stock market, when a city council considers the proposed budget for next year, when a parish committee is discussing which heating system should be installed in the new building, or when an injured child is rushed to the emergency ward at the hospital. In each case a person who may not possess any authority is the one who usually has the greatest power in making the final decision.

IMPLICATIONS

While it is still too early to predict all the implications of this trend, it is possible that the emergence of knowledge as the most important single source of power will have a greater impact on American society than any other trend identified in this book.

First of all, it means that a new class of educated persons with highly specialized areas of knowledge is coming into power. This new "ruling class" is replacing the traditional ruling class, which derived its power from property and material wealth. This means, as Daniel Bell has pointed out, that as business was the center of culture in the century following the end of the Civil War, the universities and other centers of knowledge and science will be the focal point of culture in the next hundred years.

During the past century the production and distribution of goods was the basic element in the economy. In the future the collection and dissemination of knowledge will be the focal point of life. The computer will parallel the role of the steam locomotive in the last half of the nineteenth century and the gasoline engine in the first half of the twentieth century. Or, as Peter Schrag has pointed out, educators and scientists will move into the central position of power once occupied by bankers and financiers.

A second general consequence is already visible and concerns the role of the expert in the decision making process. The traditional American ideal has been to vest the authority for decision-making in representatives chosen by the people. This produced the expression "the expert should always be on tap, but never on top." Increasingly, however, the problems faced by the members of the typical governing board have become so complex that the recommendation of the expert usually becomes the final decision. This pattern can be seen in the deliberations of the local board of education, in the decisions made by the denominational committee on pensions, in the monthly or quarterly meeting of the board of directors of the large corporation, in the formulation of American foreign policy, and in the choice of teaching materials by the parish committee on Christian education.

Power is gravitating into the hands of those who have mastered specialized bodies of knowledge. The growing power of the expert is one of the major sources of dissatisfaction, frustration, and alienation in a society that has endorsed the concept of representative democracy and is now idealizing the concept of participatory democracy.

A third important consequence of this trend has been identified by Zbigniew Brzezinski, Director of the Research Institute on Communist Affairs at Columbia University. In a brilliant article in *Encounter* (January, 1968) Brzezinski pointed out that with the emergence of what he terms "the first technetronic society" it will be possible to identify a crisis before it occurs. He suggests this will produce a shift from "post-crisis management institutions," which respond to past events, to "pre-crisis management institutions," which will have the responsibility "to identify in advance likely social crises and to develop programs to cope with them." Such a change would reinforce the power of those who have the knowledge and the capability to successfully anticipate the future.

A fourth consequence of this trend is that as more people recognize the importance of knowledge as a source of power there will be a rising demand for (a) knowledge, and (b) people who possess the knowledge that can be a source of power.

Heretofore knowledge often has been equated with formal education, education has been regarded as a source of wealth (income), and wealth has been regarded as a source of power. In the future the distinction between knowledge and education will become more apparent, and knowledge will become a direct goal of those who seek power or who seek to control the sources of power.

It is still too early to predict the entire range of consequences for the churches, but these five will illustrate some of the possible implications.

1. This new and greater emphasis on knowledge will require the churches to provide more opportunities for mid-career training and "retooling" for clergymen. This response already was visible in the 1960's in such ventures as the Urban Training Center in Chicago, Metropolitan Urban Service Training (MUST) in New York, Training in Ecumenical Action for Mission (TEAM) in Kansas City, The Clergy Intern Program in Cleveland, The Center for Parish Development in Naperville, Illinois, the Center of Metropolitan Mission In-service Training (COMMIT) in Los

Angeles, and Association for Christian Training and Service (ACTS) in Memphis.

By 1975 most of the larger metropolitan centers probably will have their own centers on the premise that the in-place aspect of the training is essential.

By 1975 the number of pastors who will feel the need for this mid-career training will be far greater than it was in 1965. The biggest change in this respect probably will come as a result of more selective recruiting and probably will include more (a) pastors of large congregations, (b) Negro pastors, and (c) denominational staff persons.

By 1975 the greatest change in these training centers will be a greater emphasis on acquiring specialized skills in communications, research, finance, planning, management, and decision making. This means a greater emphasis on what are often regarded as theoretical concepts or academic content and a reduced emphasis on field work.

2. This new emphasis on knowledge will influence the selection of denominational staff persons. Again this is a trend that has been visible for several years. Instead of an emphasis on selecting persons for denominational staff positions because they are great preachers, "successful" pastors, popular individuals, or simply because they are restless and looking for a change of pace, there is a greater emphasis on educational and technical qualifications. This trend is most apparent in selecting persons as administrators of church-related institutions, such as hospitals, colleges, and homes. It is less visible, but is present, in the current process of selecting men for regional and national positions in the bureaucracy of the churches. One of the results of this trend almost certainly will be the selection of more laymen and fewer clergymen.

3. Closely related will be the trend—and again the beginning is already visible—for a greater number of clergy-

men to leave the pastorate and move into secular positions. As pastors who are in the "restless forties" period of life are presented with the opportunity for in-service training they often will find this opens up new vocational opportunities for them. This new freedom of choice will find many ministers choosing to leave the professional ministry for a secular vocation.

One of the consequences of this trend is that some of the centers for in-service training will be identified as transition schools for men wanting to leave the ministry.

4. Another important consequence of this new emphasis on knowledge will be felt in the decision-making centers in the local church, the annual conference, the state association or convention, and the synod or district.

Traditionally much of the power held by the most influential figures in these decision-making circles was derived from seniority, age, charisma, wealth, prestige, and popularity. Tomorrow will see knowledge being as important as any of these and more important than most. As the questions facing the parishes and the judicatories become more complex, the person with knowledge, with the skill to develop an impressively documented argument, and with the capacity to identify and analyze all alternatives will have an unprecedented degree of power.

5. The influence of the churches will be determined to a substantial extent by the way they react to this trend. Two and three centuries ago the clergyman was looked upon as a leader at least in part because he was one of the few educated persons in the community.

The education, the intellectual competence, and the skill of the individuals who are identified as the leaders of the churches will be a major force in determining the influence of the churches on questions facing the larger community. Among other things this probably means that the importance of the pronouncements by a religious organization or by ecclesiastical leaders will diminish. The prophetic role of the churches and the responsibility of witnessing to the message of the gospel will be done most effectively, not by resolutions and memorials, but rather by actual involvement in the problem-solving process where knowledge is the price of admission.

6. This trend is of tremendous importance to the black churchman who is actively involved in the effort to gain a greater degree of participation for black people in the power centers of society. (See point 9 on page 148 for an elaboration of this point.)

SUGGESTIONS FOR FURTHER READING

Barzun, Jacques. *The American University*. New York: Harper, 1968.

Galbraith, John Kenneth. *The New Industrial State*. Boston: Houghton Mifflin, 1967.

Lasswell, Harold D. and Kaplan, Abraham *Power and Society*. New Haven: Yale University Press, 1950.

MacIver, Robert M. *Power Transformed*. New York: Macmillan, 1964.

Ridgeway, James. *The Closed Corporation*. New York: Random House, 1968.

Schaller, Lyle E. "Problems of Power," *Community Organization: Conflict and Reconciliation*. Nashville: Abingdon Press, 1966.

Schrag, Peter. "The University: Power and Innocence," *Saturday Review* (October 21, 1967).

Tillich, Paul. *Love, Power and Justice*. New York: Oxford University Press, 1954.

Younger, George. *The Church and Urban Power Structure*. Philadelphia: Westminster Press, 1968.

16. THE DECENTRALIZATION OF POWER

BASIC TREND

Power in the United States is being divided among an ever-increasing number of groups and organizations.

In his farewell address to the nation on the evening of January 17, 1961, President Dwight D. Eisenhower warned of the growing power and the possibility of "the acquisition of unwarranted influence . . . by the military-industrial complex."

In his book *The Power Elite* sociologist C. Wright Mills identified an interlocking circle of corporation executives, military leaders, and political figures as the real power elite. He argued that the people at the bottom of society were increasingly powerless.

Scores of other observers of the American scene have warned about the dangers of concentrating power in the hands of a few people. Critics, cynics, conservatives, reformers, revolutionaries, journalists, and adherents of the conspiracy theory of history have all come to the same basic conclusion. There is a small group of people, sometimes referred to as "the establishment," who hold nearly all power and who rule, or manipulate, the rest of the people to achieve the selfish goals sought by this elite.

Despite these dire warnings and ominous prophecies there is a considerable body of evidence to support the contention that the basic trend in American society is a decentralization of power. This view of society and of history rejects as paranoid the argument that in each community and in the nation there is a unified monolithic power structure. This point of view rejects the argument that power increasingly is being concentrated in the hands of an elite.

Among his most significant contributions as President was Harry S Truman's stubborn insistence that the military establishment must be subordinate to the civilian head of the government. Perhaps Robert S. McNamara's greatest achievement was institutionalizing the civilian control of the armed forces. The efforts of these two men first maintained and then increased the division of military power in the United States.

Eight of the twelve amendments added to the United States Constitution in the past century have broadened the area of freedom of the individual and either facilitated or required the decentralization of the power.

During the past half-century the laboring man has gained a degree of power over the determination of his compensation and working conditions that would have been described as either a dream or a nightmare in 1929, the term used depending on whether it was labor or management that was speaking.

During the lifetime of most adult Methodists the actual

power once held by a Methodist bishop has been reduced. Power in Methodism has been and is continuing to be decentralized and shared among denominational officials, laymen, and pastors.

Occasionally the analogy is developed that all or most community or national decisions are made at a single bargaining table with a limited number of chairs. If this analogy is used, the number of seats at that table has grown and is continuing to increase. During the past sixty years seats have been provided for women, the farmer, organized labor, the black man, the scientist, the poor, the educator, the consumer, the elderly, and the representatives of many other *organized* segments of society.

A more realistic analogy would be to develop the image of a community, or a nation, with many different bargaining tables. The number of these tables, or power centers, is increasing; and the number of seats at many of them also is increasing. The number of these power centers has increased to the point that most students of the process of social change agree that coalition building is one of the essential steps in achieving change.

Today there are many advocates of change who contend that the decentralization of power has reached the point in many segments of American life that it is no longer possible to build the coalition that is necessary for change without the stimulus of a crisis. A prime illustration of this thesis is local government. In most metropolitan areas in the United States the division and fragmentation of the power of local government along both functional and geographical lines has made it very difficult to secure desired improvements in such areas as the control of air and water pollution, the racial integration of the public schools, or the matching of resources with needs.

This trend toward the further decentralization of power

became highly visible during the 1950's and accelerated sharply in the 1960's.

Among the elements in this trend is the provision in the 1954 amendment to the National Housing Act of 1949, which included citizen participation as an essential part of the "Workable Program" required for urban renewal; the "Maximum Feasible Participation" phrase written into the federal anti-poverty legislation; the decision in several denominations to ordain women as clergymen; the emergence of over fifty new independent nations in the world; the inclusion of students on policy-making boards and committees in colleges and universities; Black Power; the new emphasis on collegiality in the Roman Catholic Church; the emergence and relatively rapid acceptance of the concept of "advocacy planning"; the greater participation of the client in the program designed to serve him; rent strikes; "creative federalism"; the establishment of police review boards; "participatory democracy"; the formation of councils of governments in many metropolitan areas; and the recent rapid growth of savings and loan associations. In one way or another each of these elements represented a new division of power or an acceleration in the trend toward the decentralization of power in society.

IMPLICATIONS

It is difficult to overemphasize the importance of the implications of this trend. The person who is convinced that power is being decentralized will plan and behave in an entirely different manner than will the individual who believes power is being concentrated in a single monolithic power structure.

If this identification of the decentralization of power represents a valid description of reality, and if this trend continues, it has important implications for the churchman of the 1970's.

1. For the churchman who is interested in effecting change this trend means an increasing emphasis must be placed on winning allies and building a coalition.

2. For the person who believes that the formulation of goals is important this trend means he will place a greater emphasis than ever before on involving in the goal-setting process the persons who have power to help achieve—or to help thwart the achievement of—these goals.

3. For the person who is baffled or bewildered by the increasing emphasis on lay leadership in both the Roman Catholic and the Protestant churches an understanding of the force of this trend will help him comprehend what is happening and why.

4. For the pastor serving the congregation where the administration of parish affairs reflects the trends of the times this means the day of the authoritarian leader is rapidly disappearing.

5. For the administrator of the church-related hospital, home, school, or community center this trend means he should be prepared to receive demands from both the employees and the clientele that they have a greater voice in policy-making.

6. For the middle-class white churchman long interested in the civil rights movement or in the war on poverty this trend means he cannot be as aggressive in developing policy or in formulating goals as he was a decade ago. The policy will be established and the goals will be delineated by those more directly affected.

7. For the churchman who is interested in developing closer cooperation between the government and religious organizations in such areas as housing, care of the elderly, the war on poverty, improving race relations and pro-

viding new opportunities for the black man, homes for disturbed children, improving the quality of medical care, community organization, or rebuilding the central city, an awareness of this trend will help him understand both the origins and the consequences of creative federalism. (See pages 220-29.)

8. For the political activist an understanding of the force of this trend will help him comprehend one of the most important changes in politics—the shift from the old idea that the politician in office often sought to destroy his opposition to the new practice that finds the office holder feeling constrained to financially assist his political opponent.

9. For the denominational executive an awareness of this trend will help him understand some of the motivations and implications of the growing movement toward use of the caucus in denominational decision-making.

10. For all who are puzzled and threatened by the rapid growth of various protest movements both inside and out of the churches, an awareness of this trend may be the necessary first step toward understanding why the protesters are protesting and toward distinguishing among the various sets of goals of the different groups of protestors.

11. For those who are charged with restructuring the denominational organization or for helping to make the readjustments necessitated by the merger of denominations this trend offers a basic guideline. When in doubt, move away from creating or perpetuating a powerful hierarchy and in the direction of decentralizing power.

12. For the denominations this trend also raises important questions about tactics and strategy.

Traditionally the Protestant churches have not sought to identify with any one power group. Rather the churches have sought to reach and minister to members of all groups.

Occasionally the churches have become closely identified with one of these groups—government in the colonial period, business in the late nineteenth century, the prohibition movement in the early twentieth century, and the civil rights movement in the middle third of the twentieth century. While the identification has never been complete, there have been periods when the mission of the churches was closely identified with a single group or movement. More often it has been a relatively small number of active churchmen and churches who identified with a particular group or movement. Their activity often has made the identification more apparent than real. The involvement of a few churches and church leaders in the labor movement of the 1930's is an example.

Occasionally, however, the identification with a particular group or movement has included a substantial number of national denominational leaders who influence the allocation of denominational resources. The outstanding single example of this is the identification of leaders of The Methodist Church with the prohibition movement in the first third of this century.

If "interest group liberalism" or "incorporated pluralism" is the new form of the American public philosophy, should the churches seek to become an interest group with a seat at the bargaining table? Or should the churches seek to push for the development of a new and less conservative political philosophy in America?

Should the metropolitan, state, and national councils of churches be structured to become power centers around which coalitions are built, or should they identify with one or more of these organized groups and maintain a degree of flexibility? Or should they seek to function as a separate power center?

This leads back to a more fundamental question—should the denominations and the councils of churches act as initiators or only respond to trends and forces initiated by other segments of society? Should they be change agents or only respondents to change?

SUGGESTIONS FOR FURTHER READING

Barndt, Joseph R. *Why Black Power?* New York: Friendship Press, 1968.

Carmichael, Stokely and Hamilton, Charles V. *Black Power.* New York: Vintage Books, 1967.

Carothers, J. Edward. *Keepers of the Poor.* New York: Board of Missions of The Methodist Church, 1966.

Dahl, Robert A. *A Preface to Democratic Theory.* Chicago: The University of Chicago Press, 1956.

———. *Who Governs?* New Haven: Yale University Press, 1961.

Galbraith, John K. *The Affluent Society.* Boston: Houghton Mifflin, 1958.

Jacobs, Paul and Landau, Saul. *The New Radicals.* New York: Random House, 1966.

Lowi, Theodore. "The Public Philosophy: Interest Group Liberalism," *The American Political Science Review* (March, 1967).

Miller, J. D. B. *The Nature of Politics.* Chicago: Encyclopaedia Britannica Press, 1964.

Polsby, Nelson. *Community Power and Political Theory.* New Haven: Yale University Press, 1963.

Rogin, Michael Paul. *The Radical Specter.* Cambridge: M.I.T. Press, 1968.

Rose, Arnold M. *The Power Structure.* New York: Oxford University Press, 1967.

Schaller, Lyle E. *Community Organization: Conflict and Reconciliation.* Nashville: Abingdon Press, 1966.

————. *The Churches' War on Poverty.* Nashville: Abingdon Press, 1967.

Vickers, George (ed). *Dialogue on Violence.* Indianapolis: Bobbs-Merrill, 1968.

Younger, George D. *The Church and Urban Power Structure.* Philadelphia: Westminster Press, 1963.

17. WHAT DO THEY WANT NOW?

BASIC TREND

Change and social progress will continue to produce a demand for additional changes, a reordering of priorities, and a redefinition of the goals.

"I am here to tell you that you are white racists. If you don't admit that you are racists and do something about it, you are going to have a violent bloody revolution!

"I am here to tell you that you are white racist pigs. A pig eats everything and leaves nothing for anyone else. If you don't stop acting like pigs and begin sharing with your black brothers, you are going to have a violent bloody revolution!

"I am here to remind you that when our great-grandparents were freed from slavery they were promised forty acres and a mule. The promise was never fulfilled. I am here to tell you that we are now ready to collect on that promise with interest!"

These fiery words poured from the lips of an angry young black man as he challenged 200 Lutheran ministers and their wives at the annual pastors' conference. He was responding to a questioner who had asked what message he had for the churches. The shock wave created by this part of his response rippled across the gathering and reinforced a division that already was apparent to many. Several in the audience reacted with hostility, some expressed their feelings of guilt, and others wondered aloud why they found themselves filled with feelings of hostility, fear, rejection, and guilt. A couple recognized that both the words of the speaker and the response of the audience was part of a necessary cartharsis.

Perhaps the most widespread reaction in the group, however, was expressed by one white pastor who commented, "Frankly, I resent being called a white racist pig. During the past decade I have contributed a lot of time, money, and energy to the civil rights struggle. I have taken a lot of abuse from my parishioners as I have fought for integration in the public schools, in the churches, and in many other places. Why can't you black men distinguish between those of us who are white racist pigs and those of us who have been on your side for years and who want to continue to be counted as allies of the black race? I believe I am as committed to full racial integration as any black person in this room!"

As the discussion became more heated and more confused a black clergyman stood up and declared, "You whites simply cannot understand that it's a new ball game. The game is now being played on our turf, and it's going to be played by our rules. Black people simply are not going to continue to let the white man write the rule book and decide when and where the game is going to be played!"

The events of that evening illustrate several dimensions of the racial crisis that has divided America. It illustrates the anger of many youthful black militants; the frustration of the white liberal integrationist who feels excluded from "the movement" with the emergence of the concepts of black power and "soul power"; the bewilderment of the white conservative who is convinced that tremendous advances have been achieved in race relations in recent years and who cannot understand why the Negro is not satisfied with the current rate of progress; the fear of the emotionally insecure white who is frightened by the escalation of the rhetoric; and the disapproval of the well-educated, cultured middle-class white moderate who is convinced that rudeness and violent language greatly inhibit communication and reduce the possibilities for the rational dialogue that would lead to an improvement of relations between the races.

The events of that evening also illustrate one of the most important, and one of the most complex, trends of this half of the twentieth century.

One way to describe that trend is with the phrase, "the revolution of rising expectations." In the United States, and throughout the world, millions of impoverished people, millions of people who have been discriminated against because of the color of their skin, and millions of people who have been the victims of social and economic injustice have decided they no longer will tolerate these conditions. As they achieve one victory, they do not stop to express their gratitude or enjoy the satisfaction of a greater degree of freedom or justice. Instead they define new goals and press on even more vigorously for new victories.

Their expectations—and their demands—rise at a faster pace than society moves to make the adjustments necessary for the fulfillment of these expectations. As progress is made in reducing the injustices the gap between the actual conditions of the society and the expectations of the oppressed does not narrow. Instead it continues to widen. This baffles many of those outside the struggle—and also some of the allies—who cannot understand why progress produces increased dissatisfaction.

A Negro lawyer living in a $40,000 home in a racially integrated suburban community explained this point to two of his white friends with these words. "You fellows think that because you white people have stopped lynching niggers, because you let people like me go to your private universities, because you let me and my family live in a nice home in a fine suburban community, and because you let my children go to the same school that your kids attend, you think that black people like me should bow, say 'thank you' and continually show our gratitude. You think we should stop talking about 'black power' and stop pushing so hard. Well, just let me tell you right now that we aren't going to stop pushing, we aren't going to forget about black power, and we aren't going to de-escalate our demands until we are accepted as full and equal partners in every facet of this society and until you treat everyone of us as human beings!"

The same point can be illustrated by looking at the war on poverty. It appears inevitable that the present paternalistic and dehumanizing welfare system in the United States will be replaced by some form of guaranteed annual income, probably before 1975. It also appears inevitable that this will not reduce the level of discontent among those living at or below the poverty line. It will not quiet the crisis of injustice and discrimination. This will not come until poor people are accepted everywhere as equals and as persons and are treated with the dignity and respect due every one of God's children.

Another dimension of this same basic trend can be illustrated by the paradox that as people come close to achieving a goal they frequently make radical changes in their goals.

Again the racial crisis supplies a relevant illustration. All through the 1950's and for the first half of the 1960's the dominant goal of the civil rights movement was racial integration. The goal of both Negro and white leaders was integration—in housing, in public accommodations, in education, in employment, and in every other facet of society.*

In the second half of the 1960's the goal was changed. As the black clergyman quoted earlier said, "It's a new ball game. The game is now being played on our turf, and it's going to be played by our rules."

While a great many Negroes continued to believe, and to act on, the old theory that the ultimate goal of equality could be achieved by first seeking integration, an increasing number of black people decided that the first goal must be full equality. This meant equal participation in the community decision-making process, in the marketplace, and in the distribution of the fruits of an affluent society. Out of this grew the cry of "Black Power!"

This change in goals confused a great many white liberals

---

* In retrospect it appears that the one possible exception to this was in the churches. The white churchmen in the civil rights movement also wanted to achieve actual racial integration in the churches. Some of the Negro leadership apparently placed a greater emphasis on achieving the *opportunity* for racial integration in the churches than on actually achieving integration in congregational life. An obvious reason for this was that the institutional life of the Negro church and of the Negro denomination was threatened to a far greater extent by the one-way street integration of that era than was the institutional life of the white church and white denomination.

who had been active participants in the civil rights movement. They found this was a new ball game and that it had a new set of rules. One of the rules was that a person could not be a manager, coach, or captain unless he was black. In most of the games he could not even be in a starting lineup unless he was black. To those who had battled vigorously for years for racial integration this was a strange turn of events.

This trend reflects an important change in the source and distribution of power in American society. While the complete details of this trend cannot be defined at this point in history, it does help support the contention that some of the previously powerless segments are now gaining power.

One of the consequences of this redistribution of power is a new demand for changes more extensive than those articulated earlier by a first, smaller band of reformers. Another consequence is that the new holders of power will demand—and secure—a voice in the community decision-making process. Perhaps the most significant consequence of this trend is that the people most affected by the goals of new reform movements are demanding—and securing—the power to reformulate the goals of the movement. Those most affected by the reforms in public programs are demanding and securing the right to help draft the new programs.

Just as the working man of the 1930's demanded and secured a voice in determining his compensation and in establishing the conditions under which he labored, so the black man today is demanding a voice in establishing the goals of the racial revolution, and the public welfare recipient is demanding a voice in determining the nature of the system used to redistribute the wealth of an affluent society.

Just as the goals of organized labor have changed in the

past three decades, so will the goals of the "black revolution" and the "welfare revolution" change in the coming
years.

IMPLICATIONS

Before one can begin to predict and appreciate
the implications of this trend it is necessary to point out
that the impact of this trend is and will be felt in all segments of society, not just in the struggle for racial justice
and in the war on poverty. It is most obvious in these two
areas. The ramifications of this trend in these areas are
widespread and highly visible.

This general trend of an escalation of expectation with
an accompanying redefinition of goals can be detected in
all facets of society. It can be seen in what the school expects of the student; in what the parishioners expect of the
pastor *and in what the pastor expects of his parishioners;*
in what a profession such as medicine, the law, or the ministry expects of the practitioner; in what the general public
expects of *both* the public and the private sectors of the
economy; in what the child expects of his parents, and in
what the parents expect of the child.

Another type of illustration of this same trend can be
seen in what the college or university expects of the student. At Harvard, for example, the person who would have
ranked in the middle of his class in 1956 would have stood
at the very bottom in 1964 with the same level of achievement. The ferment on campuses all across the country in
recent years demonstrates that the student also now expects
more of the school than did the student of the early 1960's.
Here again the person to whom the program is directed
wants a voice in formulating the goals and establishing the

structure of that program. There is a remarkable similarity between the revolt of the university student and the protest of the welfare recipient.

Within this context there are several implications for both the parish and the church at large.

1. The new emphasis is and will be on participation. The pastor, the denominational executive or the lay leader who seeks and secures the involvement of the people who will be affected by the program that is being devised will be a much more effective leader than the one who goes ahead and unilaterally defines purposes, sets goals, and determines structure.

2. The individual, whether he is a leader or a participant, who can accept the demand for changes in goals as the program proceeds and who can understand the demand for additional changes as change occurs will be a more effective member of the team—and also will lead a happier life.

3. The pastor who sees in this trend a tension-producing force in society and in his parish and who can respond effectively in helping people understand the source of these tensions will be a most valuable member of society.

4. This trend will continue to produce new tensions among both the critics and the supporters of the struggle for racial justice and the national campaign to eliminate poverty. As this occurs in a society that is increasingly compartmentalized along racial, economic, and social lines (see Chapter 12), the churches will have a larger role as channels of commuications, as interpreters of social change, and as agents of reconciliation.

5. Perhaps most important of all, as riots and rebellions continue to occur the churches can be constructive forces in what follows.

The churches can help people see the consequences of various courses of action—of how the best ally of the black racist is the white bigot, of how complete capitulation may be as destructive as unrestrained suppression, of how polarization is an ally for those who would destroy this society rather than a means of preserving it. The churches can help people see that the winning of a tactical victory—perhaps by brutally breaking up a protest demonstration—may produce a strategic defeat. The churches can help people understand why the young people who are subject to the military draft must have a greater voice in the administration of the draft.

The churches can help direct the formulation of national goals—the construction of a multiracial society that includes the right of equal participation; the creation of a society in which human dignity is a fact and not a cliché; the evolution of a community in which the recipient of services has a greater voice in the administration of the institutions that provide those services; the development of a nation in which social justice is the goal of everyone, not just of those who are denied justice.

The churches can help people understand that change naturally produces a demand for more changes, and that goals must be re-evaluated and reformulated by those most affected by the movement toward fulfillment of the original goals.

SUGGESTIONS FOR FURTHER READING

Barndt, Joseph R. *Why Black Power?* New York: Friendship Press, 1968.

Brink, William and Harris, Louis. *The Negro Revolution in America*. New York: Simon and Schuster, 1964.

Graubard, Stephen R. (ed.). "The Negro American," *Daedalus*, The Journal of the Academy of Arts and Sciences (Fall, 1965 and Winter, 1966).

Hadden, Jeffrey K. *The Gathering Storm in the Churches.* Garden City, N.Y.: Doubleday, 1969.

Ramsey, Paul. *Christian Ethics and the Sit-In.* New York: Association Press, 1961.

Report of the National Advisory Committee on Civil Disorders. New York: Oxford University Press, 1968.

Schaller, Lyle E. *The Churches' War on Poverty.* Nashville: Abingdon Press, 1967.

Tucker, Sterling. *Beyond the Burning.* New York: Association Press, 1968.

Vickers, George (ed.). *Dialogue on Violence.* Indianapolis: Bobbs-Merrill, 1968.

Wildavsky, Aaron. "Black Rebellion and White Reaction," *The Public Interest* (Spring, 1968).

PART FIVE

THREE TRENDS IN THE RELIGIOUS ARENA

18. CHURCH AND STATE: THE CRUMBLING WALL*

BASIC TREND

In recent years the churches in the United States have been developing a closer relationship to government, especially to the federal government, and this trend will continue.

In 1802 Thomas Jefferson sent a letter of commendation to the Baptists in Danbury, Connecticut, in which he used the phrase, "a wall of separation between church and state."

Today commentators on the church-state issue frequently single out two issues—the prayer in public schools decision of the United States Supreme Court issued in June, 1963, and the taxation of church property—and use these to il-

* Portions of this chapter are adapted from an article "The Challenge of Creative Federalism" that appeared in *The Christian Century,* May 10, 1967. Permission for reprinting is gratefully acknowledged.

lustrate their thesis that the wall between church and state is being reinforced.

A more careful analysis would suggest that two things are happening to Mr. Jefferson's famous wall. At the one end a mixed crew of clergymen—including a large number of Baptist ministers and Jewish rabbis—public officials, atheists, agnostics, and taxpayers are working diligently to strengthen and raise the height of the wall.

All along the wall a much larger number of people are busily knocking holes in the old masonry and gradually tearing down what is clearly a crumbling wall. This group includes administrators of church-related institutions, civil rights leaders, Baptist ministers, young clergymen who are social and political activists, federal officials, builders, financiers, speculators, lawyers, and a miscellaneous assortment of Protestant and Catholic pastors and denominational executives.

As they watch these proceedings several scholars smile knowingly and comment, "Some of these fellows don't realize that the original reason for building that wall was to keep the government from interfering with the freedom of religion. Now some of these men are trying to strengthen the wall to prevent any form of cooperation between the government and the churches."

In fact it is ridiculous to talk about complete separation of church and state in the United States. Scores of actions have been taken by government that recognize the existence of institutionalized Christianity. Many of these have aided the churches both institutionally and in terms of their mission.

These actions include exemption from the general property tax for houses of worship and, in some states, for parsonages; hospital and military chaplains paid by the government; the placing of "In God We Trust" on coins; the addition of "under God" to the pledge of allegiance; the issuance of a special Christmas commemorative postage stamp each year for the past several years; Sunday closing laws; the classification of contributions to churches as tax-deductible items for income tax purposes; the special tax treatment accorded clergymen on housing allowances; special postage rates for church-sponsored periodicals; the exemption of church-owned businesses from corporate taxes; and the request for clergymen to open public meetings with prayer.

In recent years this list has been lengthened, and many of the additions include the payment of large sums of public funds to church-sponsored and church-related programs and institutions. This list includes the Economic Opportunity Act of 1964; the Elementary and Secondary Education Act of 1965; the Hill-Burton program, which over a 20-year period provided a half billion dollars in construction grants to church-owned hospitals; the various housing programs that provided both capital *and operating funds* for church-owned and operated housing projects; federal grants for both construction and instructional purposes to church-owned colleges and universities; the grants of public funds to church-owned and operated nursing homes; and state and local governmental payments to church-owned and operated homes for children.

These grants mark a new alliance between the government and the churches. This is not only a new alliance between church and state, it also marks a new era in the manner in which the federal government goes about the task of achieving certain national goals.

This can be seen most clearly by contrasting the operating techniques of the New Deal and those of the Great Society. In the 1930's nearly all the major social welfare programs were conceived, created, financed, and administered by the federal government; only a few were channeled through existing state and local governmental agencies. But during the 1960's a radically different approach was developed. In his 1966 State of the Union address to Congress, President Johnson urged the nation to "move on to develop a creative federalism to best use the wonderful diversity of our institutions and our people to solve these problems and to fulfill the dreams of the American people."

The political attractiveness of this "creative federalism" concept is illustrated by *Life* magazine's endorsement of it. In a speech in Washington, Richard Goodwin, former aide to presidents Kennedy and Johnson and later an adviser to both Senator Eugene McCarthy and Senator Robert Kennedy and the man who coined the phrase "creative federalism" called for a decentralization program under which the federal government would provide the funds and guidelines, while the local community would take responsibility for action and implementation. *Life* found Goodwin's concept to be in "accord with much Republican thought" and urged the Republicans to adopt it as party policy.

The political appeal of the concept was not dimmed by the 1966 election returns. Immediately following that election, several congressmen—among them liberal Democrat Henry J. Reuss and conservative Republicans Charles E. Goodell, Gerald Ford (House Minority leader), and Melvin R. Laird (chairman of the House Republican conference)—reviewed Walter Heller's 1964 proposal that the federal government make massive financial grants to the states. While those proposals differed in detail, both recognized and accepted the central idea of dependence on the federal government to mobilize the necessary money and dependence on the states for administration and programs of implementation. The basic differences between the Republicans and Democrats in this matter arise over (1) whether the federal government should provide guidelines directing how the grants are to be used, and (2) the role of the state governments in relationship to local agencies. These differences were emphasized in the 1968 presidential campaign and in the early days of the Nixon administration. On the other hand, the 1968 campaign and President Nixon's statements have underscored the basic agreement that this is a pluralistic nation and that there is a high degree of interdependence between the private and the public sectors of the economy.

An examination of recent legislation and of the practices pursued in implementing it suggests that the call for "creative federalism" is more than rhetoric. The federally financed war on poverty leans heavily on allies from the nongovernmental sector of the economy. Private corporations (such as Litton Industries) have been engaged to operate Job Corps centers, churches have entered into contracts to operate Head Start programs, private universities have secured federal grants for community organization efforts. Other private agencies are using anti-poverty funds for a variety of programs.

The federal government now is urging private organizations and groups, as well as state and local governments, to become active partners in the drive to achieve a better society. In effect, Uncle Sam is saying to prospective partners: "I will provide a large share of the necessary money and dictate the general policy guidelines if you will agree to supply the managerial capability to implement these programs in the local community."

Clearly, this offer is directed to the churches and to church-related institutions also. In 1956 the court decision in *Schade v. Allegheny County* removed one of the last major barriers to participation by religious organizations in federal schemes. In this case the court ruled that maintenance of neglected children is not a charity or benevolence but is rather the government's duty, and that the payments made by the government to cover the costs of such maintenance do not constitute aid to a denominational or sectarian cause. However, this ruling was beclouded when the U.S. Supreme Court refused to review a Maryland judicial decision declaring *state* grants to church-related colleges unconstitutional.

But the question for the churches today is not whether creative federalism is constitutional, nor whether the invitation by the federal government includes the churches; the question is how the churches will respond to this invitation.

Why Does Uncle Sam Want This Alliance?

It may be helpful at this point to examine some of the reasons *why* the churches are being invited to become partners in solving the nation's social problems.

First, the churches have a history of favorable response to government invitations to join in national causes. The churches vigorously supported the federal government during World War I and, somewhat less emphatically, during World War II. Moreover, the churches and their related institutions have accepted government assistance on many occasions during the past two decades. This assistance has taken the form of grants for hospital construction, tuition payments to church-related colleges and seminaries under the G. I. bill, and payments for the care of dependent children. For several years, for example, many church-related children's homes have been receiving 50 to 80 percent of their operating costs from government agencies. Logically, therefore, in any attempt to create a broad-based coalition for solving the social problems the church would be considered a potential ally.

Second, there now exists a severe shortage of managerial capability in our society, a shortage graphically illustrated by the "pirating" of executives in private industry, by the difficulty both presidents Johnson and Nixon had in filling top executive posts, and above all by the haphazard progress in the war on poverty. It has been easier to get Congress to approve an appropriation than it has been to find in the local community an agency to administer the funds effectively and responsibly.

Third, and closely related to the second reason, is the fact that the rapid expansion of the population in urban areas has almost overwhelmed local government with problems of growth and survival. One result is that the local governments do not have enough managerial talent to administer the implementation of the new programs being developed in Washington.

Fourth, and perhaps most important, is the belief shared by many government officials that the Christian churches have valuable resources to contribute to the national effort to solve certain immediate problems—e.g., their concern for the individual as a child of God, their emphasis on compassion and on love as motivating forces, their endless drive for social justice. Many government officials are convinced that these resources mean that the churches are uniquely qualified to operate a home for neglected children, a center for senior citizens, a housing project for low income families, an educational program for four-year-olds, or a pilot program to reduce juvenile delinquency.

As churchmen struggle to make the appropriate response to the challenge of creative federalism, however, they find themselves divided on several issues, the most prominent of which is the church-state question.

Three Responses

Examination of various situations in which this question is being faced suggests that three types of answers are emerging. At one extreme is the strict separationist theory—more frequently and vigorously articulated than followed. In general, those most distant from the actual point of decision-making tend to be the strongest proponents of strict separation. At the other extreme are the policy makers for church-related institutions such as homes, hospitals, and colleges. Many of these have concluded that the only way their institutions can survive is by abandoning the strict separation principle and accepting government aid. As a result of these conflicting views severe tensions have developed within the various denominational families, especially in Baptist circles. Several Baptist institutions have actually severed their ties with the church in order to be free to accept federal aid. More commonly, the denominations have attempted to develop a compromise acceptable both to the strict separationists and to the administrators who demand a policy statement that is relevant to contemporary conditions.

Perhaps the most creative statement of this type to date is the one adopted by the Lutheran Church of America at its annual convention in Kansas City in mid-1966. This statement, while rejecting the absolute doctrine of separation, calls for the *institutional* separation of church and state but at the same time recognizes the need for *functional* interaction of the two. Such functional interaction could permit church-related institutions to accept government payment for services rendered to individuals. In early 1968 The United Methodist Church produced a similar but somewhat more restrictive policy paper that defined the goal of "interaction with independence." Policy statements of this nature are acceptable to churchmen who see the churches as logical partners in creative federalism, but are still unacceptable to the Protestants who fear that any deviation from strict separation opens the door to government subsidy of Catholic schools.

A second divisive issue among churchmen concerns the role of the churches in the effort to solve domestic problems. Should the churches emphasize services and program, or should they give first priority to social action? If the latter, should they concentrate on cooperating with the government in implementing programs in the fields of health, education, welfare, and housing; or should they focus their energies on helping the victims of social injustice to organize for self-help? Hundreds of church-related institutions have agreed to become partners in creative federalism. Hundreds of churchmen, however, contend that the churches' resources are more desperately needed in social action, community organization, the civil rights movement, and the pursuit of social justice.

The tensions arising from these differences of opinion are sharpened by the fact that while the federal government is making more and more money available for service programs, it is increasingly reluctant to provide funds for social action and community organization efforts. Churchmen who favor service programs in social welfare and housing find it relatively easy to secure large federal grants. By contrast, those who favor an approach directed toward changing the basic social structures are discovering that it is very difficult to secure funds for anything resembling political action.

A third issue grows out of the nature of the problems involved. Many churchmen insist that social and economic problems can no longer be ignored. But since—so they argue —history makes it plain that the efforts of private enterprise cannot eliminate these social ills, the basic issue reduces to a simple question: Should responsibility for all these problems be turned over to the government to finance and administer, or is it better to maximize the participation of private organizations, including the churches? Which is preferable—socialism or pluralism?

Many Christians think that this formulation oversimplifies the problem and ignores possible alternatives. They insist that no massive effort on the part of either government or churches is needed; strong emphasis on thrift, hard work, self-reliance, and honesty, coupled with an expansion of employment in the private sector of the economy and the maintenance of law and order, will eliminate a large proportion of our social problems. Most of these people, of course, would disagree with the basic assumption that this nation is now affluent enough to deal with these social ills. (See Chapter 10.) Discussions in local churches and in those denominational meetings that include a large number of lay delegates make it amply evident that the lay leaders of American Protestantism have many more reservations about creative federalism than do the clergymen who administer those church-sponsored programs which could be strengthened by federal funds.

This split is closely related to the contention that surrounds the issue of financial mobilization. Many churchmen argue that if each affluent American Christian would give a tithe of his income *to the churches,* the churches would have plenty of money to operate all their institutions and to build many more. Mathematically, this argument is sound; realistically, it will not hold water. The fact is that today the federal government alone has the power to mobilize the vast sums necessary for education, subsidized housing, medical care for the old, and so on. To suggest that the churches should play a major role in solving the problems created by white racism and poverty *and* pay all the costs thereof is to indulge in utopian fantasy and, worse, to obscure more basic questions.

Another problem—one that has been largely overlooked—is the geographical and denominational organization of the churches' response should they consent to become active partners in creative federalism. Currently, most church-related institutions are set up on a denominational basis, with both the clientele and the middle-class governing board drawn from a large geographical area such as a conference, diocese, synod, or association. But the emphasis in creative federalism is on finding partners at the neighborhood or community level. Here again one can see a manifestation of the trend toward decentralizing power and extending the right of self-determination. (See chapters 14 and 16.)

To respond on these terms, the churches probably will have to shift from a denominational to an interdenominational or interfaith organization. Such a shift will entail a reduction in the power of the denominational representatives and an increase in the degree of participation by persons living in the neighborhood or being served by the program. It also will entail a very high degree of participation by lower-income people, by Negroes, by women, and by other individuals who are unable to make large financial contributions to the institution or program. All these developments are bound to generate tension and to produce some very divisive reactions.

Some churchmen, for example, will view the invitation to join this partnership as a sinister plot to make the churches a tool of the government. They see the government making the policy decisions and setting the priorities while the churches are exploited to achieve political goals. While there may be grounds for such doubts and fears, the churches would be well advised to comprehend the goals of creative federalism fully before they decide what to do. These goals have been clearly articulated in an address by Senator Edmund S. Muskie of Maine:

> Creative federalism, as I see it, involves both co-operation and competition of ideas and performance between all levels of government, between government and private organizations, and between individuals. It is a partnership in the common objective of building our country and improving the lives of our citizens; but it involves a matrix of independent powers and differing methods of achieving this objective. Creative federalism does not make the national government the senior partner in this partnership . . . (it) is based on the traditional American habit of sharing responsibility.

Only time will tell whether this glowing description is accurate.

While American Protestantism has not yet given a clear-cut answer to the invitation to become a partner in creative federalism, literally hundreds of churches and church-related institutions have responded affirmatively. Most of these responses have come from established organizations. The list includes the local churches that have shared in Head Start, state councils of churches that have used anti-poverty funds to enlarge their ministries to migrants, church-related hospitals that have received Hill-Burton construction grants, denominations that have accepted federal funds for housing projects for the elderly, and church colleges that have sought and received federal grants and loans.

Or to put it more simply, the churches are responding affirmatively to Uncle Sam's invitation to come over and help tear down Mr. Jefferson's wall.

IMPLICATIONS

The most serious implications of this trend for the churches can be stated by a brief question. Who is setting the priorities for the churches? One of the grave dangers is that the lure of federal matching funds *will continue* to influence the ordering of priorities in the churches just as it is in state and local government. There still remains a vast difference in the attitude of federal officials who see the churches as a valuable ally in the effort to achieve certain national goals and the attitude of many officials in state and local government who see the churches as owners of huge quantities of tax-exempt property. The general argument over church-state relations should not neglect this distinction.

Taken together these two observations raise a third question. In the event a major policy change in Washington results in cutting off the federal funds, who will be left holding the bag? This is a serious question for the church-sponsored organization that develops an extensive program and builds up a large payroll. If the federal contribution suddenly is reduced, will the denominations be expected to make up the difference?

Finally, concerned churchmen need to ask whether a complete tearing down of the wall may jeopardize the freedom of the churches. The wall was built originally to insure the freedom of religion. Will its destruction place this freedom in jeopardy?

SUGGESTIONS FOR FURTHER READING

Balk, Alfred. *The Religion Business.* Richmond: John Knox Press, 1968.

Bennett, John C. *Christians and the State.* New York: Scribner's, 1958.

Curry, James E. *Public Regulation of the Religious Use of Land.* Charlottesville: The Michie Company, 1964.

Guild of St. Ives. *A Report on Churches and Taxation.* May 6, 1967.

Hefner, Philip J. (ed.). *The Future of the American Church.* Philadelphia: Fortress Press, 1968.

McGrath, John J. (ed.). *Church and State in American Law.* Milwaukee: Bruce Publishing Company, 1962.

Panoch, James V. and Barr, David L. *Religion Goes to School.* New York: Harper, 1968.

Schaller, Lyle E. "Uneasy Alliances," *The Churches' War on Poverty.* Nashville: Abingdon Press, 1967.

Smith, Elwyn A. "Should Church Assets and Income Be Taxed?" *The Christian Century* (July 17, 1968).

Tussman, Joseph. *The Supreme Court on Church and State.* New York: Oxford University Press, 1961.

19. THE GROWTH OF THE THIRD FORCE

BASIC TREND

The sects and denominations outside the mainstream of cooperative Protestantism have become the fastest growing religious bodies in the United States.

Four denominational "families"—Baptist, Methodist, Lutheran, and Roman Catholic—include more than two-thirds of the residents of the United States who claim a religious affiliation. A score of large "mainline" denominations account for two-thirds of the 70,000,000 Protestant church members in the United States. Statements such as these underscore the dominance of a relatively few denominations among the several hundred religious groups in this country.

Statements such as these also obscure one of the more interesting contemporary trends in the American religious arena. This is the combination of a sharp decline in the rate of membership growth in many of these large denominations and the high rate of growth in many of the smaller pentecostal, adventist, and holiness groups, and in some of the independent and sectarian churches.

In a recent 15 year period the Roman Catholic Church increased its membership in the United States by 37 percent, all Protestant bodies reported a combined increase in membership of 31 percent—and the Churches of Christ reported a 135 percent increase.

In the early 1940's the Jehovah's Witnesses had approximately 100,000 members. In 1968 they were over the one million mark, although one-third of these members were outside the United States.

From 1953 to 1965 The Methodist Church reported a 13 percent increase in membership. The Wesleyan Methodist Church reported a 38 percent increase for the same period, and the Mormons reported a 66 percent increase for the same 12 years.

In general terms the larger mainline denominations reported membership increases averaging 1 or 2 percent a year for this period, while the holiness, pentecostal, and adventist groups and some of the sects reported increases averaging 4 to 12 percent annually.

The contrast became even sharper during the middle 1960's as the average annual increase in several of the larger denominations such as The United Methodist Church, the United Presbyterian Church in the U.S.A., and the United Church of Christ dropped below 1 percent and occasionally was a minus figure. During these same years the churches outside the mainstream of cooperative Protestantism continued to grow at rates that usually ranged between 3 and 8 percent per year.

In an article in *Life* back in 1958 Henry P. Van Dusen described the emergence of this growing group of Christians

COMPARATIVE RATES OF MEMBERSHIP GROWTH

Denomination	Membership		Percentage Rate of Growth
	1953	1965	
Assemblies of God	370,118	572,123	55%
Christian Reformed	186,526	272,461	46%
Church of Jesus Christ of the Latter Day Saints	1,077,285	1,789,175	66%
Church of the Nazarene	249,749	343,380	38%
Church of God (Cleveland, Tenn.)	131,623	205,465 (1964)	55%
The Methodist Church	9,151,524	10,331,574	13%
Church of God in Christ	338,304	425,500	26%
Pentecostal Holiness	43,943	56,506	44%
Pentecostal Church of God in America	38,000	115,000	203%
Pilgrim Holiness	30,592	56,506	85%
Seventh Day Adventist	260,742	364,660	40%
Southern Baptist Convention	7,883,708	10,770,573	36%
United Presbyterian, U.S.A.	2,721,222	3,304,321	22%
Wesleyan Methodist	34,955	48,326	38%

SOURCE: *Yearbook of American Churches.* New York: National Council of Churches in Christ, 1954, 1955, 1956, 1966, 1967, 1966.

who identified with neither Catholicism nor with the mainstream of cooperative Protestantism. He used the term "Third Force" to identify these clusters of churches and sects that were emerging as rivals and competitors of traditional Protestantism and American Catholicism. He estimated that 60 Third Force denominations in the United States had a combined membership of 7 million.

During the next decade some of these groups either virtually or completely disappeared, several passed from the sect to the church stage of their institutional life cycle, and others entered into an era of unprecedented growth.

There are at least three aspects of this trend that merit

the interest of most churchmen. These may be described by the three words *who, where,* and *why.*

1. Who? While detailed statistics are not available, it appears that most of the new members of the Third Force churches are members of minority groups, are drawn from the lower income groups, or are young (age 18-40) persons who have moved from a rural to an urban community.

This generalization is based on personal observation and a scattering of reports and studies. It should be emphasized, however, that not all the new adherents fall into these categories. Visits to these congregations reveal a surprising number of college-trained persons, many with graduate degrees. Each congregation usually includes at least a sprinkling of middle-class, economically and socially conservative persons who have left one of the larger mainline denominations.

2. Where? While many of the churches in the Third Force appear to be strongest in the rural areas and small towns of the South, they can be found in increasingly large numbers in the central city, in the suburbs, and out on the rural fringe of the large metropolitan centers of the north and west.

3. Why? There is no simple answer to the question about why the Third Force is growing so rapidly. Among the more obvious probable reasons are (1) the individual who joins one of these congregations finds himself a member of a warm fellowship in which there is a sincere expression of concern for him as a person; (2) the person who feels alienated from society or lonely or apprehensive often can find a comfortable and reassuring sense of companionship within one of these congregations; (3) rarely is there a display of "social distance" between the laymen and the clergymen that might repel some members; (4) the congregations tend to be small, and small congregations tend to have a much better record on evangelism, outreach, and the recruitment of new members than do large congregations.

In an article in the *Journal for the Scientific Study of Religion* (Spring, 1968) Luther P. Gerlach and Virginia H. Hine suggest five factors that help explain the growth and spread of Pentecostal churches.

1. They have a reticulate or network type of organization that provides a supportive infrastructure without the handicaps of most bureaucracies.

2. Recruitment of new members usually follows existing kinship and friendship lines and is carried out on a face-to-face basis.

3. The new recruit usually is involved in a commitment act or experience that reinforces his allegiance.

4. The change-oriented and action-motivating ideology encourages and enables the new member to understand the beliefs of the church, to accept them without reservation, and to feel that the strength of his belief gives him a sense of personal worth and power.

5. A sense of persecution or at least a perception of opposition from "outsiders" helps to strengthen the fellowship and bind the members into a more closely knit body.

IMPLICATIONS

Of all the trends identified in this book some of the implications of this one are both the most obvious and the most puzzling.

Several observers contend that with the passage of time the churches in the Third Force will become institutionalized and more closely resemble the mainline denominations. As this happens communication will improve, and cooperation will increase. Proponents of this point of view point to the Church of God (Anderson, Indiana) and the Church of the Nazarene as examples of denominations that are in the advanced stage of this process.

Others see the beginning of an era of infiltration of the beliefs and practices of the Third Force into the mainline denominations. The most common illustration offered to support this argument is the spread of *glossolalia* or speaking with tongues. Both laymen and clergymen in the Protestant Episcopal Church, several of the Lutheran Churches, The United Methodist Church, and other mainline denominations have publicly experienced this phenomenon.

In more specific terms there are six other implications of this trend that should be of interest to readers of a volume such as this.

1. While the percentage figures of growth are impressive, in actual numerical terms all but a few of the denominations in the Third Force are relatively small. Their combined size is probably no more than the combined size of The United Methodist Church, the two largest Presbyterian bodies, and the Protestant Episcopal Church.

2. By far the greatest impact of the Third Force has not been in the United States, but rather in the overseas mission fields, especially in South America. Whether this represents an alienation from their own culture as William G. McLoughlin asserts, or whether it truly represents an expression of evangelical fervor is hard to say. Regardless of the motivation, the Third Force churches currently have nearly twice as many missionaries serving abroad as do the 20 largest mainline Protestant denominations in the United States.

In many of the mission fields there is severe, often bitter, competition between representatives of the Third Force and the missionaries sent by the traditional Protestant denominations.

3. In many respects the growth of the Third Force ap-

pears to be a current running against the tide. This can be seen in the position of leaders in the Third Force on biblical scholarship, on social issues, on race, on economic questions, and on politics. For example, several different sources indicate that about two-thirds of the ministers in the Third Force voted for Barry Goldwater in the 1964 presidential election. More opponents than proponents in the battle for racial justice or in the war to end poverty have come from the churches of the Third Force.

4. Many Protestant churchmen have shown little or no interest in the growth of the Third Force. Instead of worrying about this split between the two branches of American Protestantism they have devoted their time and energy to building bridges between the mainline Protestant churches and their Roman Catholic neighbors. This pattern stands in sharp contrast to the attitudes of the generation of clergymen who were confronted with the fundamentalist controversies of the 1920's.

5. Perhaps the most significant and the most overlooked of the implications of this trend is that the appeal of the Third Force churches is not limited to "the disinherited and the maladjusted" as once was thought to be the case. Today the churches of the Third Force are appealing to significant numbers of college students, young married couples, and middle-income white-collar workers.

6. In addition to reporting a comparatively high rate of membership growth, the denominations in the Third Force are pursuing an extremely aggressive program of new church development.

In 1960, for example, the Methodists, the three largest Lutheran bodies, the two largest Presbyterian denominations, and the Disciples of Christ started a combined total of 589 new missions. By 1967 the interest and the apparent need for new church development by these denominations had dropped, and they started a combined total of only 241 new congregations. In 1966 and again in 1967 the Churches of God alone launched 700 new congregations. While such denominations as The United Methodist Church and the United Presbyterian Church in the U.S.A. have been reporting a small annual decrease in the number of congregations, the denominations in the Third Force are reporting an annual increase in the number of congregations that average about 3 or 4 percent per year.

Among other things this means that in the next few years the 20 mainline Protestant denominations that include 65 percent of all Protestant church members in the nation and account for 30 percent of all Protestant congregations will establish perhaps 25 percent of all the new Protestant congregations. The denominations in the Third Force, which today include less than one-fourth of all Protestants in the United States, will organize one-half to two-thirds of all new Protestant congregations that will be launched between 1965 and 1975.

SUGGESTIONS FOR FURTHER READING

Furniss, Norman F. *The Fundamentalist Controversy*, 1918-1931. Hamden, Conn.: Shoe String Press, 1963.

McLoughlin, William G. "Is There a Third Force in Christendom?" *Daedalus* (Winter, 1967).

Maslow, Abraham. *Religions, Values, and Peak-Experiences.* Columbus: Ohio State University Press, 1964.

Nichol, John T. *Pentecostalism.* New York: Harper, 1966.

Pope, Liston. *Millhands and Preachers.* New Haven: Yale University Press, 1942.

20. CONNECTIONALISM AND DENOMINATIONALISM

BASIC TREND

Connectionalism will continue to replace congregationalism in the polity of American religion, and this will continue to enhance the role of the denomination.

While traditionalists still tend to describe the basic forms of church government as episcopal, presbyterial, and congregational, a new form of church polity is beginning to dominate the American religious scene. This new form of church government can best be described by the word *connectionalism.*

Methodists have long used the word "connectional" to describe their denominational structure. In simple terms it means that all the churches and members of Methodism are interrelated. Each minister, while a member of an annual conference, is considered a member of the whole church. Every member is considered to be a member of the total church, not simply a member of one congregation. Every local church has a clearly defined tie to all the boards and agencies of the district, the annual conference, and the general church.

For many years The Methodist Church, the United Presbyterian Church in the U.S.A., the Presbyterian Church U.S., and the Evangelical United Brethren Church stood out as the four best examples of a connectional church. One of the reasons why the merger of The Methodist Church and the Evangelical United Brethren Church was so easy to consummate was that both were connectional churches.

In recent years connectionalism has become more popular. In part this may be associated with the general trend toward centralization. In part this growing popularity of connectionalism is a pragmatic response to the stresses and strains placed on the contemporary church at both the parish and the denominational levels.

During the 1960's the connectional ties binding the local church to the presbytery and to the national church have been reinforced in both of the two large Presbyterian communions. The current emphasis on "interdependence" in the Protestant Episcopal Church is another illustration of the increase in connectionalism. The restructuring that has changed the Christian Church (Disciples of Christ) from a brotherhood into a denomination is another illustration of the same trend.

In July, 1962 four Lutheran bodies merged to form the Lutheran Church in America. This was more than an absorption, however, of three smaller groups by the much larger United Lutheran Church in America. It was also a reorganization that replaced the old ULCA—which was really a loose federation of synods—with a connectional church. At about the same time the merger that produced the new American Lutheran Church strengthened the degree of connectionalism in that branch of the Lutheran family.

Likewise the merger of the Evangelical and Reformed Church with the Congregational Christian Church that produced the United Church of Christ also was an ecclesiastical reorganization. The new denomination has a connectional character far stronger than could be found in the old Congregational Christian Church.

While stronger in practice than in theory, a growing sense of connectionalism can be detected in the American Baptist Convention and especially in the Southern Baptist Convention.

Signs of the continued growth of connectionalism can be seen in nearly every merger and reorganization that involves a mainline Protestant denomination. The "new look" in Roman Catholicism in the United States also has reduced the isolation of the parish and increased the sense of connectional ties in that organization.

Signs of the continued growth of connectionalism can be seen in the increasing use of reversionary clauses that state that the property of the local church shall revert to the denomination if no longer used for the designated purposes.

Other illustrations of this trend can be seen in the changes in pastoral placement that increase the influence of the denominational office; in the increase in the number of denominational specialists assigned to work with local churches; in the relegation to a local denominational judicatory, such as a district or a presbytery, of the responsibility for implementing certain specialized issue-centered ministries that previously would have been handled by a local church; in the organizational changes that result in metropolitan councils of churches, which formerly were in fact councils of congregations, being reconstituted as "councils of denominations"; in the shift that has transferred much or all of the responsibility for new church development from the local church to a regional judicatory or to an agency of the national church; in the many special denominational fund-raising drives in 1968 and 1969 developed to raise money locally to help the denomination respond *through the boards and agencies of the national church* to the urban crisis; in the development of new curriculum and materials for the church school by the national boards of the denominations; and in the continued trend to place the responsibility for the administration of foreign missions work in a national board.

A review of the changes occurring in the denominations that have long had a connectional polity, such as the Presbyterians and The United Methodists, and of those that have begun to move in this direction more recently, such as several of the Baptist groups, the Disciples of Christ, the Church of the Nazarene, the Lutherans, and the Unitarians suggest this trend toward a growth in connectionalism will continue.

IMPLICATIONS

The implications of this trend can be divided into four categories for discussion purposes, although there is some overlapping of the categories.

For the Denominations

Connectionalism strengthens the denomination and enhances the role of the denomination. Connectionalism increases the already pronounced tendency of American churchmen to identify themselves with a denomination and to maintain that denominational affiliation as they move from one community to another. (Contrary to the popular stereotype, most church members in the United States are members of the same denomination in which they were reared. In a survey originally made in 1952 and replicated in 1965 eight out of ten people said they were members of the same denomination in which they grew up. About eight of ten husbands and wives belong to the same denomination as their spouse.)

As Andrew Greeley has pointed out, denominationalism in the United States has produced the organizational vitality that is the base for religious scholarship, for the internal self-criticism that distinguishes the churches from other institutions in this country, and for the prophetic voice that is without parallel in any other nation. The continued growth of connectionalism undoubtedly will strengthen all three of these characteristics of institutionalized religion in the United States.

For both the denomination and the individual churchman one of the most important implications of this trend will be in the division of responsibility and of authority. Already in those denominations where connectionalism is the strongest, it is possible to discern a distinctive pattern.

It appears that the responsibility for general policy formation, for general supervision and review of past performance, for the allocation of resources and for the assignment of priorities among general goals is being lodged in the larger judicatory that includes one or more states—such as the conference in The United Methodist Church or the synod in the United Presbyterian Church in the U.S.A. The responsibility for implementation, the power to assign priorities among projects, and the veto power increasingly are being lodged in the smaller administrative unit—the district or the presbytery. As connectionalism becomes a stronger force in other denominations this same pattern probably will emerge there.

For the Ecumenical Movement

On both a national and worldwide scale the expansion of the ecumenical movement has been heavily dependent on the growth of denominationalism. It is reasonable to expect that as the growth of connectionalism continues to enlarge the strength of the denominations this in turn will strengthen interdenominational cooperation and the whole ecumenical movement.

More specifically this probably will be most visible in four areas.

1. There will be a continued movement toward the merger of denominations from within the same denominational family—e.g., the Lutheran Church in America with the American Lutheran Church, or The United Methodist Church with the Christian Methodist Episcopal Church, or the Presbyterian Church, U.S. with the United Presbyterian Church in the U.S.A. Since most mergers of denominations are the product of the desires and efforts of a relatively few denominational leaders, rather than the result of a call from the grass roots, the strengthening of the denomination will make it easier to achieve the merger of denominations. Since 1925, 133 denominations in 21 countries have merged to form 38 new denominations. The next 45 years probably will see an even larger number of denominations involved in mergers.

2. There will be an accelerated movement to increase interdenominational cooperation and the implementation of joint projects. The two most common forms of this probably will be (a) the cooperation of two or three denominations in jointly staffing regional judicatories, and (b) the joint financing of specialized ministries on issues and to the structures of societies. In addition there will be an increase in the number of jointly sponsored new missions, in the number

of congregations sharing building facilities with other congregations, and in the number of jointly sponsored experiments to discover new forms for the parish.

3. There will be a continuation of the recent trend to use the denominational judicatory rather than the local church as the basic constituent unit for interdenominational cooperation.

4. There will be an increase in the number of denominationally financed ecumenical agencies that devote a substantial proportion of their resources to a criticism of denominationalism and to describing the shortcomings and the failures of the denominations.

For the Parish and the Parish Pastor

The most highly visible change for the layman and the parish pastor that is being produced by the rise of connectionalism is in pastoral placement. Instead of the pastor being called as the result of a unilateral action by the congregation, or being appointed in a unilateral action by a bishop or the cabinet, a new system is emerging. In this system, which still has not been officially formalized in most denominations, the congregation, or more specifically a specially designated committee from the congregation—one or two denominational officials and the pastors who are available for a call or an appointment—jointly work out the arrangements. Typically the denominational officials exercise a screening power in reducing the number of possibilities to a relatively small list, while both the congregation and the pastor may exercise a veto power.

With slight changes and some exceptions this description of the process of pastoral placement now describes how pastors and churches are matched in many of the denominations that use the call system and in most of the denominations where pastors nominally are appointed by a bishop.

The growth of connectionalism will see this method of pastoral placement being used more widely in more denominations.

A second implication that will be felt in the parish is that as the denomination is strengthened the rift between many laymen and the denomination will be widened as change-oriented agencies of the national church issue what are viewed as radical pronouncements and engage in what are viewed as radical ventures by the conservative, status quo-minded layman.

The short-term result, already apparent in hundreds of parishes, will be to place the pastor in the tension-filled position of trying to interpret, explain, and defend the actions of the denomination while at the same time trying to placate the aroused layman.

The long-term result will be to increase the number and the influence of laymen in the denominational decision-making process. This will be initiated and supported as an expression of participatory democracy, as a means of curbing the power of ecclesiastical bureaucrats, and as an effort to extend the ministry of the laity. It also will be supported by those who see a need to increase and strengthen the channels of communication between the denomination and the parish. The nature of the selection process, however, is such that this development will have little impact on either the decision-making process or on the nature of the decision.

A third implication for the parish is that the isolation of the parish will diminish as more members see themselves not only as members of a specific congregation, but also as members of the denomination and the larger church. This will come most quickly in those denominations where there is a strong regional judicatory, such as the district in The United Methodist Church or the Association in the United Church of Christ. It will come more slowly in denominations without such a strong regional judicatory, such as the Lutheran Church in America or the American Lutheran Church. To a very significant extent it already has happened in the two largest Presbyterian bodies where the presbytery fills this role.

As this happens it makes it easier to mobilize resources across parish lines to enable the churches to respond to the challenges posed by a complex society. As this change occurs it also strengthens the role of the regional judicatory (and increases the demand for one where a viable unit does not exist).

A fourth, and perhaps for the local church the most important, consequence of the growth of connectionalism is that more parish churches will have a *nearby place within the denominational family* to which they may turn for specialized help on specific problems. The increase in specialized staff on the denominational payroll and the growth in importance of the regional judicatory are two of the characteristics of connectionalism. As more denominations move toward a connectional polity this means more parishes will have more resources available to them. (One by-product of this is that the role of state and local councils of churches and other interdenominational agencies will have to be redefined. Some of the services they once supplied will be taken over increasingly by the denominations.)

Finally, the rise of connectionalism means a decline in congregational autonomy. Among other things this means that there will be a curb on the survival instinct that has motivated many congregations to move from the difficult challenges of the inner city to the green pastures of suburbia. Or, to make this same point in more affirmative language, the rise of connectionalism increases the possibility that the resources of the churches will be assigned to the places where the need for service is the greatest rather than to the places where chances for survival and institutional growth are the most promising.

For the Future

Will connectionalism be an obstacle to change, or will it facilitate probable changes in organization, structure, and polity? The answer to this question depends to a substantial degree on the nature of the changes that may come, although connectionalism does have a commendable degree of flexibility.

It appears that the next major organizational trend in the ecclesiastical institutions in this country will be a movement toward a decentralization of authority, especially in the responsibility for implementation of programs designed to achieve national goals. This trend is already apparent in the policies of the federal government that are embraced within the concept labeled "creative federalism." (See pages 220-29.)

If the denominations adapt the concept of creative federalism to their polity and structure it will mark a major shift from the recent pattern of increased centralization of power at the national level. It will increase the opportunity for and the practice of democracy in the administration of denominational affairs. It also will expand the possibility of connectionalism emerging as the new American polity.

SUGGESTIONS FOR FURTHER READING

Cavert, Samuel McCrea. *The American Churches in the Ecumenical Movement 1900–1968.* New York: The Association Press, 1968.

———. *On the Road to Christian Unity.* New York: Harper, 1961.

Harrison, Paul M. *Authority and Power in the Free Church Tradition.* Princeton: Princeton University Press, 1959.

Haselden, Kyle and Marty, Martin E. (eds.). *What's Ahead for the Churches?* New York: Sheed & Ward, 1964.

Lee, Robert. *The Social Sources of Church Unity.* Nashville: Abingdon Press, 1960.

Maring, Norman H. and Hudson, Winthrop S. *A Baptist Manual of Polity and Practice.* Valley Forge: Judson Press, 1963.

Marty, Martin E., Rosenberg, Stuart E., and Greely, Andrew M. *What Do We Believe?* Des Moines: Meredith Press, 1968.

Mead, Sidney E. *The Lively Experiment.* New York: Harper, 1963.

Niebuhr, H. Richard. *The Social Sources of Denominationalism.* New York: Henry Holt and Company, 1929.

Pfeffer, Leo. *Creeds in Competition.* New York: Harper, 1958.

Schaller, Lyle E. "Connectionalism: The New Polity," *The Christian Century* (July 1, 1964).

INDEX